JT hel...
BOOK - C
VALDESE, NC! I MISS NC!
ALSO HOPE THAT You
WILL BE ENCOURAGED BY
WHAT You READ.

THIS
AT

Heading Toward the Final Finish Line

by

Rrrick Karampatsos

Your FRIEND ~

XULON
PRESS

Heading Toward the Final Finish Line
by Rrrick Karampatsos

Printed in the United States of America

ISBN 978-1-60647-961-2

www.xulonpress.com

Table of Contents

An Invitation

The picture on the cover of this book shows one finish line of many crossed by Rick despite his being told many years ago that he would never walk correctly again - which certainly implied that he would not be a competitive runner. Rick seemed to have had more accidents and injuries than there were races entered and completed – certainly more than enough to stop most people.

Since two days after his 1964 graduation from Pentucket Regional High School in West Newbury, MA many injuries have found their way into hospital records. You will read about many of Rick's accidents in this book. Some were very serious; none kept him from moving toward his goal. Rick will also tell you about how his Lord and Savior, Jesus Christ, touched his heart and his body over and over again enabling him to find both spiritual and physical renewal.

Rick wore a number of club singlets with pride over the years including those of the following organizations: Salisbury Rowan Runners, Concord Runners Club, The Athletes Heart –Team 413, Marathon Maniacs, Tampa Bay Runners, the 50 States and DC Marathon Group, 50 States Marathon Club, the 4 His Temple running club, and the Christian Runner's organization.

Drawing from the strength of his Christian faith and accepting the forgiveness of past mistakes, Rick got himself on course and in his unique way proclaims the *'Good News'* of the Gospels. Each race across America became a podium whereupon Rick ministered and shed the light of the *'Blessed Hope'* (Titus 2:13) with his running.

Rick invites you to sit back and be a part of his adventures which he has chronicled in a series of articles he has written along the way; or as he says, as he is "heading for the final finish line". Whether you are a walker, a new runner, an ultra racer, or maybe even a *'maybe someday I will try!"* person, he wants you to share the joy he experienced as he witnessed to and encouraged others during his miles of training, traveling, and racing across America.

Janice Coulter

Acknowledgments

I have been encouraged by a number of people since I went on disability in 2002. I felt a need to run and to stay in shape. Little did I know that our Lord had big plans for me and by His grace, would place some key people along the course of my life. These wonderful people helped mold me into a person to be used by Him in a ministry of encouragement - by way of running races and writing about the experiences.

The Lord called forth people from my church fellowships, as well as runners who helped me improve and stay healthy, and from other areas of my life. I want to give thanks to those who helped me in three special areas.

Spirit*ually, it is my Lord and Savior, Jesus Christ* to whom I give thanks and praise. If He had not healed me those two times that I will tell you about later, I would still be in a wheelchair. Moreover, if He had not loved and died for me, I would be on a course to hell.

My son, Pastor Jason, and his wife Jennifer, blessed my ministry with a blog - www. june3rd.com/blogs (now – www. therrrick.com). Thousands of people across the country and the world have read it. Their continuous prayers and belief in the ministry made a tremendous difference for the spiritual success of it.

For ***running support,*** one man stands tall above all others, Ed Frye — the *'Ironman'* from Kannapolis, NC. He helped me to become the runner that I am today with great training tips, with encouragement during races and at the Y.M.C.A. (where he is a lifeguard), with help purchasing the correct items from his other place of work (Phidippides Sports Center) and by always being an incredible friend.

The last area has to do with ***my writing.*** I had given up on it. A wonderful woman, who I will just refer to as *'Song Bird'*, from Gold Hill, NC helped me rediscover the gift that I had misplaced during so many hard miles in my life.

I have been blessed with a ministry and with running adventures that I would have never dared dreamed about because of *her gentle encouragement,* Ed's hard driving coaching, and the caring of others the Lord drew into my path.

To this short list, I add a *'thank you'* to my sister Janice for providing corrections and helpful suggestions for this book.

I pray that as you read this book you remember, as I do, the people I mentioned who help make it possible. I also pray that you will have and appreciate such friends as you head TOWARD THE FINAL FINISH LINE.

Dedication

"As long as Moses held up his hands, the Israelites were winning, but whenever he lowered his hands, the Amalekites were winning. When Moses' hands grew tired ...Aaron and Hur held his hands up—one on one side, one on the other—so that his hands remained steady till sunset. So Joshua overcame the Amalekite army with the sword... Moses built an altar and called it The LORD is my Banner. He said, 'For hands were lifted up to the throne of the Lord.'" (Exodus 17:11-12)

I was in spiritual warfare financially and emotionally with my ministry, was tired physically, and was spiritually weakened. I knew that I needed help to continue in this battle.

The verses above came to me as I reflected on my situation. The church body at Life Point Community (www.life-point.tv) where I attend believes that *no one should stand alone.* I called upon my close friends, **Jim Klein** and **Gary Parramore,** to hold me up in prayer. Jim, as the leader of the Life Group (Real Men©) called upon the men to join in with him and Gary to pray. They were by my side lifting me up so I could continue to - not only be helped - but also, be able to continue to help others through my ministry.

It is to these men and men like them that I dedicate this book.

Foreword

Heading Toward the Final Finish Line

*Running
with
perseverance
the
race marked out
for us-
pressing on
towards the goal
to win the prize
for which God has called
me
Heavenward in Christ Jesus.*

(Heb. 12:1c & Phil. 3:14)

~~~~~~~~~~

RELAX, READ and REMEMBER
the
pleasures and pains
of the
RACES RUN, STATES CHECKED OFF,
and the
MILES RECORDED
that wore out sneakers
BUT NOT
THE SOUL.

My Top Three Priorities

These are the top three priorities I hold firmly in my heart when I write, do my training, and run marathons around this great country.

Encourage the Christians
along my path
get the religious
on the
right course
and,
draw the
spectators
into the *Heavenly race*
with my witness of Joy
and
by displaying the *symbols of my faith*
- *the cross and fish.*

chr.tripod.com

Financial 'FOOT'- note

A portion of the sales from this book will go to support:

TEAM 413 - www.team413.org and the Christian Runners
Organization www.ChristianRunners.org

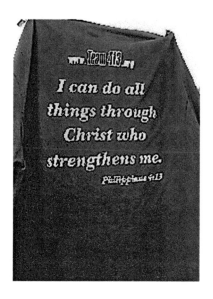

Introduction

Heading Toward the Final Finish Line

We will all cross many finish lines in our lifetime and be rewarded for the effort. The wording will vary. Runners will obviously call it just that – a finish line. However, it is that and a lot more for runners and for many others. It might be referred to as a *crowning touch, pinnacle or completion* after a hard struggle doing 'something'. Maybe it did not take much of an effort to reach the end of what you were doing. Whether it was a race with a trophy to hold after seemingly endless hours of training and sacrifices, or the wrap-up of a home project, the achievement was yours to claim (and maybe share).

Those trophies, achievements or the money earned, although accepted at the time as a worthwhile investment of your pain, expense, and time, are going to fade. Not just in your friends' memories, - but in yours. They will be soon overshadowed by new races and new personal goals. Sadly enough, few of our achievements will be remembered after we die.

I want us to think about the effort, expense and pain we expend preparing for the final finish line. Do we draw a line at some point as to what is needed to be a Christian and the importance of *'heading toward the final finish line?'*

Have we forgotten what Jesus taught in Matthew 6:19-24 about the treasures stored here on earth that will get rusty or stolen? And, what about the cost of being a Christian in this present society?

Within these pages, you will be the judge of your own personal logbook and spiritual journal. You will be able to more clearly ask and answer what shape you are in for the last few steps, those moments crossing over into eternity. I pray that you will enjoy laughing at yourself, even with (or at) me as I share some valuable lessons I have learned while reflecting upon my running and racing adventures.

The challenges are not over. The spiritual warfare on and off the road to Heaven is still very much before us all. Let us joyfully continue with prayer and bible study. A great place to get a refreshing study is on the web at www.oneplace. com. The study that I love to listen to is **Running to Win** with Dr. Erwin W. Lutzer. You also can listen to the broadcast on the web site or on a local Christian radio station that has Moody Broadcasting.

Remember, the headlines are already written for all who cross the glorious heavenly finish line. We, the victorious saints - **W I N!**

The SRR Singlet

The Salisbury Rowan Runners (SRR) singlet showed up in another picture in another article written about an SRR member on June 21st, just a few days prior to the China Grove Challenge. The Salisbury Post ran the following article; the member was Rick Karampatsos.

asiphoto
The Charlotte Observer 10K Race Fest 04/21/2001
(78th of 1,219)

Rick Karampatsos is another member who takes pride in the fact that he is a member of the Salisbury Rowan Runners. As a matter of fact, he takes pride in the fact he is a runner at all, since had it not been for a couple of big miracles, he would not even be walking.

In 1982, while at work, Rick received a massive electric shock, which left him unable to work for two years. Then in 1984, he fell off a roof breaking two vertebrates. Both times, doctors expressed doubt that he would ever walk correctly again. But he did. Now he's not only running, but also winning trophies and PRs – and he never hesitates to give God the credit for healing him both times. He will tell you in a heartbeat Who he owes his life to.

Rick joined SRR last year and has quickly become an active member. His participation in the 1000 Mile Club keeps everyone wowed since he records over 300 miles a month. Rick received his 100 Mile award back in May and continues to run strong. SRR members are so sure that he will reach 2000 miles this year, the trophy has already been ordered!

SRR's 3,000 MILE CLUB MEMBER

"Little did we know when we started the 1000 Mile Club last year that we would not only have members reaching 2000 miles in a years time, but also 3000 miles! As of November 29th [2001] Rick Karampatsos had done a total of 3,300 miles and the year is not over! With Rick averaging over 300 miles a month, it is expected that by the end of this month, Rick will have run over 3,000 miles! Rick! You make it seem so easy!"

— David Freeze

I logged 3,514 miles my first year in the SRR club.

Looking back at the many years of seemingly endless accidents, I am now blessed to see God's plan for me unfolding. I will continue to lift Him in praise, trust Him in the deepest of darkness, and serve Him with the gift that has been placed within my body.

Every day, before my first step is taken, starts with me on my knees in thanksgiving. I am *prayed up and then show up* to be an ambassador for my Lord whether I go to the streets to run, to the local YMCA to exercise, to work, or to do my daily errands. My testimony is for all who will listen. The fact that I am running at all is proof that Jesus is still in the healing business! The fact that I am testifying and running all the way **Toward the Final Finish Line** is proof that Jesus has made me His own and has set the course for the balance of my life.

"Park the Car in Harvard Yard"

Most of us have heard someone try to repeat a joke they had heard only to kill the punch line and have the listeners wondering what was supposed to be funny. When a Yankee tries to speak a word with the letter 'r', well, it has an effect similar to the person who can not make a joke work to get a laugh. The listeners are pulled toward the humor of how the words are pronounced rather than the sentence itself. Some things are better heard than read. "Park the Car in Harvard Yard" read here will not produce the same effect as if I said it aloud to you. My Boston Yankee accent is lost within the written words. When I say certain words with an r, the location of the r within the word can make difference. If I am writing that life is sometimes like a *'road race'* – the **r** seen twice does not achieve the humor as if I said it aloud.

This may be a good place to share the story of how my name was changed to **Rrr**ick from Rick. It is a bit silly maybe - but I have had fun with the new spelling. And, perhaps, you have looked at the spelling and wondered about it. A friend of mine wrote a note at the end of a greeting card and spelled my name with the letter **r** three times. She wrote that it was to make up for the **r** that I do not pronounce! I continued to have fun with the name and had a vanity plate done for my car that reads **RRRICK'S** on it!

I could speak (or write) about the sensation of running a marathon to someone who is a non-marathon runner, or even to folks who do not take part in the sport at all and I will never come close to successfully expressing the emotional and physical experiences of those 26.2 miles (especially crossing the finish line!). Spoken with a *'Yankee'* or with any other accent, the experience will not be fully understood. It is clearly a situation that the listener (or reader) has to experience firsthand.

~~~~~~~~~~~~~~~~~~~~~~~

We now need to press forward to some very important truths. Please follow me closely here and do not let your thoughts *drift off course.*

I went back to this article after its completion and made some changes because one of my editors made observations about how my words in certain parts might discourage versus encourage some of my readers. The points that I feel led to share as I write are very important. I also believe the feedback I received on this section was helpful in that it allows me to clarify my views in order to avoid having other readers experience similar doubts about my message.

Although I hope all readers will benefit from this book, it is to Christian runners that I have primarily targeted my words. I do not expect them to 'do as I do' step-by-step. No, I am just trying to encourage them in the faith and with Scripture to *'step out in faith'* with the power of the Holy Spirit to more openly witness not only in actions but with words of testimony. Our actions speak volumes – true. However, runners who are not saved often show Christian-like qualities. We need to point to the source of our salvation and freedom – **Jesus Christ.**

For over thirty years I have seen and been personally blessed by physical healings. You will read about this elsewhere in this book. I have openly expressed my love for Jesus as my Lord and Savior during these years. As I traveled across America doing marathons, I shared the "Good News' with many people and the reasons for my excitement at being a Christian and, I have pointed out the major differences from my past 'religious' life. Many have looked at me with empty eyes and some even have said that they did not believe that Jesus healed me. Many Christians do not understand the joyful excitement of talking about my faith – some have said that I should not talk about it at races with nonbelievers. The articles on my blog (www.therrrick.com) and the ones in the running club newsletters have sometimes drawn negative remarks.

But I press forward in love knowing that those of you whom I am able to encourage, and the others that you will encourage, will in turn be able to reach still others with the 'Good News'. You will see runners that I will not. I am only one. Some of you will be touched by the power of the Holy Spirit while reading this or when hearing my voice out on the course, and will reach out to many others that I will never be able to reach, never mind, even see!

"Perhaps the race course is not where a person focused on breathing and other elements of running can slip into a conversation about God."

That comment is one I received on my first draft. It is a comment with which many might agree. However, I have seen my approach work during many marathons. The other runner may not be able to talk as easily as I do – but will ask me to keep on sharing and he or she will listen. The Christian runners even seem to get excited and discover *hidden strength come from within* them during this time of fellowship! I pass them one of my cards and many e-mail me with positive reports.

"If someone has not been led by the spirit to witness, I don't know that it is up to other people to do the leading. And, if they do not want to witness so publicly, that too is a personal choice – and doesn't

mean they aren't witnessing in other ways. Not everyone has the outgoing personality to do this.

Can you imagine a shy Christian running up to another runner as you do? It would be a shock to his/her system.

It is my understanding that we are all called to be witnesses, but are not all gifted with the tongue of an evangelist – hence there are many more ways of displaying our faith through how we live and treat others."

I understand, and yet, my heart is saddened that some Christians feel they can not witness by talking openly to strangers about Jesus. I strongly believe that *those of us who can do this need to share the excitement of it* with them and *guide them as we move forward to witness* at races not only to other Christians, but to the untold numbers who are not Christians.

These comments brought back a conversation with a friend with whom I shared a room at a race. He was upset with me for talking with his Christian and non-Christian friends about Jesus and what He has done in my life.

I shared scriptures about the Great Commission and others in line with this need to share our faith. He said that he would think about it.

He did! He called me a few days later and shared how the Holy Spirit had been working in his heart about our conversation. He thanked me and asked me to stay at his house for a few days. I did and we ran a marathon there, and YES – we shared with people there about Jesus. I was also blessed to be able to talk to and encourage his family, a neighbor and a few of his running club members.

This speaks to the point in that last comment from the editor. This man did not feel led. The Holy Spirit used me to open the door to 'thinking about it'. It was the Holy Spirit that ministered to him AFTER I shared.

And yes, I can imagine others running up to strangers as I do if and when the Holy Spirit empowers them!

There will be some that are not gifted as an evangelist. True. However, there will be more if we allow the Holy Spirit to use us to encourage the gifts that are hidden and waiting to be used to glorify our Lord! If only one, that one may lead many to *'the final finish line'!*

How a person hears makes a big difference in the acceptance of the Word as truth. I am not talking about hearing it from a person with a 'Yankee accent' or with a 'Southern drawl'. *"...the Word of God is living and active. Sharper than any double-edged sword, it penetrates even to dividing soul and spirit, joints and marrow; it judges the thoughts and attitudes of the heart."* (Hebrews 4:12)

The way we live, along with the sharing of our testimony and the Word of God will draw many to Christ.

The following is a closing note that was given with the suggested changes and 'things for me to think about'.

> *"I believe our Christian obligation is to use what-ever our personal gift is so that when nonbelievers see our behavior or hear our words, they can not stop themselves from saying Praise the Lord!"*

To that, I say, "Praise the Lord and Amen!" (Smile)

We have been blessed with the gift of running; some of us are able to run marathons and perform triathlons. We need to openly give Him the praise and honor due Him for this gift! That will be a great witness and open up doors of conversation. Amen and Amen.

> *"... I want you to get out there and walk—better yet, run!—on the road God called you to travel. I don't*

want any of you sitting around on your hands. I don't want anyone strolling off, down some path that goes nowhere. And mark that you do this with humility and discipline—not in fits and starts, but steadily, pouring yourselves out for each other in acts of love, alert at noticing differences and quick at mending fences." (Ephesians 4:2-3 MSG)

"Reckless words pierce like a sword, but the tongue of the wise brings healing." (Prov. 12:18)

The following from 1 Cor. 9: 24-27 points to the power of commitment.

"...Run in such a way as to get the prize. Everyone who competes in the games goes into strict training. They do it to get a crown that will not last; but we do it to get a crown that will last forever. Therefore, I do not run like a man running aimlessly; I do not fight like a man beating the air. No, I beat my body and make it a slave so that after I have preached to others, I myself will not be disqualified for the prize."

As runners, we are at different levels of training and ability. As Christians, we are at different places in our faith and are blessed with different gifts of the Holy Spirit. Our understanding of spiritual truth grows as we study the Word of God. Moreover, as we allow the Holy Spirit to guide us in the truth, that truth will set us free (John 8:31–36). Free to serve Him with our gifts by the power of the Holy Spirit.

A person has to live out the experience to better understand it. No writings, sermons or conversations can completely express the feelings and knowledge – I can only try to draw others to a closer understanding and desire to experience sharing the "Good News" firsthand.

~~~~~~~~~~~~~~~

I pray that all of you will allow the power of the Holy Spirit to enable you to join in with Paul:

"I'm not saying that I have this all together, that I have it made. But I am well on my way, reaching out for Christ, who has so wondrously reached out for me. Friends, don't get me wrong: By no means do I count myself an expert in all of this, but I've got my eye on the goal, where God is beckoning us onward—to Jesus. I'm off and running, and I'm not turning back" (Phil. 3:12-14 MSG)

Never Alone

Have you ever finished a race with a very good pace time, or maybe, *'just finished the race'* - then gone over to the table, turned in your number information, continued to get your refreshments – and only had thoughts about *'your'* efforts? Maybe you went back out to run for a while to cool down before the winners (*maybe you!*) were announced. Did you spend any time thinking about **your team members?**

"Team members – what team members?"

I believe that as runners we are all on a team. Maybe you have taken that **extra step** and have joined a local running club. Great! However, you are still wondering about being on *'a team'*. I will explain.

As runners, we are an extension of each other. Many believe (runners also) that runners are people who *'just do it alone'*, *'run for the freedom of the sport'*, *'take a single action'* – and so forth. This line of thinking may be true in some ways, but not completely. Let me ask you this: *"When was the last time you helped out with a race that was sponsored by your club?"* **Ouch! Don't stop reading – please.**

Without the helpers, the best efforts toward organizing a race will fail. Runners remember how races were organized. They mentally and emotionally remember how **their day went** from the pre-race and start line, during their race journey, to how they were treated at the finish line and following events. What they recall will determine if they will return the following year. We must not forget the impact on the running club both financially and to its reputation.

As difficult as it is sometimes to explain the reasons that you run to non-runners, it is often as difficult to share the joy of working to put on a race together. To borrow a well-known NIKE ® phrase –you have to *'Just Do It'®* to better understand. I pray that those of you who have not done so yet will treat yourself to that pleasure soon.

When I first began to run after forty plus years of *'just jogging'* - even that was just once in awhile – someone asked me if I belonged to a running club. I quickly answered that I was not a real runner. That week I joined the Salisbury Rowan Runners' club. I strongly recommend this club for all runners in the Salisbury, NC area. They guided me and encouraged me in many ways. I dare say that without their fellowship, especially the club president David Freeze, I might not be running at all. Club membership is that important.

At first, it was tough to be a helper and not run in the race! Then I found ways to help before and after some of the races and still be able to run the race! I have to admit that when I worked the finish line, I felt proud of myself and learned to respect what has to happen at the finish line to have it be a successful event.

With club members and family, you are **never alone**!
That's my son Phillip standing with me after the race.

Now back to being a team member. An athlete in any sport needs help from others. It may come in the form of doctors, trainers – and yes, good friends. It comes from people you do not even know! It comes from the people who designed your sneakers and your running hat, from those who write articles to teach you to run better – the list does go on and on! **YOU**, as a runner, are **never alone.**

The people who line up along the streets during a race are an important part of me being able to continue (especially while running marathons). A friend answered one of my e-mails (in which I'd shared about an upcoming race) with - *"I may be miles away in body, but will be there on the sidelines in spirit to pray and cheer you on!"* I know that there are many *'unseen faces'* praying for me as I run my races – I am *'never alone'* during those miles.

The next time you go out for your run, I trust that you will feel confident knowing that like faith, you do not have to see in order to believe that others are by your side *'mile after mile'* cheering and helping you reach your goal. **I am proud to be a runner and a team member** in this great sport of running. **Together** we are all winners and share the common trophy called - *friendship.*

That Hill

I am not surprised at how I feel or how people are reacting to me today. For a long time, in fact as long as I can remember, I knew about **'that hill'** – and how difficult it would be to get up it. Well, today I am ascending it and, even with no surprises, I feel almost defeated and unprepared. I have never been part of a finish like this. Not to sound like I am complaining, but really, the hill is tough enough – it is added cruelty to have to finish at the top of it. But I must continue forward.

World of Color©
The Bear (Grandfather Mt.) 7th Annual
Linville, NC 7-12-2001

Slowing down, I feel like the weight of the world is upon me. My legs feel like they are about to collapse under me.

Looking at the people who line the way does not offer any needed strength - the crowd seems different from others that I have seen. I feel alone among so many. I hope that my heavenly Father is still proud of me although I do not see Him; I know that He is watching me.

I feel like I have been preparing all my life for this course. In fact, it has been less than four years. Not much further and it will be finished. It will be recorded that I was a loser. What is that saying, "the last shall be first"? No, that does not apply here.

I just saw a familiar face in the crowd crying - I feel bad about that sorrow. I wish that my friends were around to comfort her and to help her and others understand why I am doing this; why it seems today that I am not the man they thought I was. Yesterday they were all cheering for me. Today some are looking at me as a failure and others see me as a great disappointment. However, I do not hold it against them; they just do not understand.

When I feel that I might be too weak to continue during a race or in my Christian daily walk, and am in need of help physically and spiritually, I draw from the following Scripture: *"...righteousness from God comes through faith in Jesus Christ to all who believe...all have sinned and fall short of the glory of God, and are justified freely by his grace through the redemption that came by Christ Jesus. God presented him as a sacrifice of atonement, through faith in his blood."* (Rom. 3:22-25 in part).

I know that I was a helpless sinner and was going to hell. I now also know that by His stripes, I am healed! This hill and every hill that I need to go up remind me of the victory Jesus made possible because He did make it to the top of His hill and died for me upon that cross. Jesus had Simon from Cyrene to help him get up *and continue.* I have the Holy Spirit and I will rise to finish what I started. *"I can do all things through Christ who strengthens me."* (Phil. 4:13)

This is more than the story of Jesus - it is my story expressing how I think Jesus felt going up the hill to Calvary. Visualizing this way reminds me of the price of sin and how much Jesus loves us.

Please read the above one more time before continuing with the rest of this article.

Because of what Jesus did for us, there is always help to get up when we fall into sin as Christians. We can confess, repent, and then continue on the course to the eternal finish line. Moreover, because of His grace, everyone can join in at any point in life and join the redeemed Christian believers.

Because I know this truth, I am able to continue in my weakness and in my pain (pain that I consider a badge of honor). Each step is in faith and I praise Him for the opportunity to glorify Him with my running.

The next time you feel as if you are going up a tough hill in life, or when you are physically running up one in a race, remember that Jesus has already gone before you. During your difficult races on the toughest hills, mentally and spiritually place yourself on *'that hill'*. Run in appreciation of what Jesus did.

"It is finished" – *all you have to do is praise your way toward the finish line!*

Team Omni Health

Just pretend for a moment that you work for Omni Health and you receive a call from a man who states – *"I need to have an appointment right away; I hurt my back."* You answer that you could set up an appointment for him within a few days, but he quickly states that it needs to be almost right away because he is planning to run a marathon in two days and needs to fly to Philadelphia the next day! How would you handle that conversation? NO PROBLEM if you were on the staff team at Omni Health.

Within the hour I was at their office – and even with such a strange request – they were very kind, helpful, and showed concern about me being able to run that marathon. Within a few hours, I had an answer for my situation and some pain relief. I learned that I could run with no further harm to my present injury. An appointment was made for the following week and I was then on my way back home to prepare for my trip.

When I returned for my second appointment, they welcomed me with smiles and congratulated me on my finish of a *3:53:52 chip time.* That was my first marathon. From that day on, I have been blessed with 'follow up treatments' and pleasant fellowship. Both have been a tremendous help to my body, health and running efforts.

Every visit has worked well for me, including the chiropractic treatments, the great massages, my time in the exercise area, and my visits with Dr. Van Ness who kept up on my progress and constantly offered excellent advice on what I should (and should not) do during my training workouts. The office personnel could melt the heart of any person and they are 'worth the visit' by themselves alone. They truly have healing powers that add to the services there!

Now, **in 2001** at the age of 57, I joyfully testify to logging over 6,000 miles and 60 races with 53 wins in my age division. I owe much of my success to Omni Health, and rely on them to be *'the force'* that keeps me running healthy. I believe that my Lord set them on my path to guide me medically. Their Christian witness is beyond any price that could be paid anywhere in the area. They know and apply the following truth: *"For physical training is of some value, but Godliness has value for all things, holding promises for both the present life and the life to come."* (I Tim 4:8)

I pray that the Omni Health staff will continue to serve 'The Great Physician', Jesus Christ, by helping people recover from pain while helping them move more smoothly toward that 'heavenly finish line'.

Island Photography©
Philadelphia Marathon 2001
Chip time: 3:53:52

Pride, Pain and Pleasure
November 2002

As I sit here at my desk in pain (*hamstring again*), I will share my thoughts about a question that was upon my heart after a race this past month up in Galax, VA. The question is: *Is there a difference between 'pride' and 'proud' and how do they apply in this sport of running?* I am no expert on the English language, so please bear with me as I try to get some basic points down and follow them with a lesson I have learned.

Interestingly, dictionaries define PRIDE and PROUD in 'both' a negative and a positive light. The difference between the words is basically in usage – noun versus adjective. As to the meanings: on the negative side, it is possible to have an undue sense of one's own superiority which pretty much translates to arrogance or conceit; but there is the positive view which speaks to having a proper sense of personal dignity and worth; being justly proud for having done something extremely well. There's the English lesson. On to my story!

A few caring **Salisbury Rowan Runners** club members were concerned that I ran too many miles (3,600+ last year) and started the races too quickly (5:58 last week at the Woolly Worm Woad Wace during my first mile). They also spoke of running too many races (around 60 since I joined **SRR** in 2001) as well as talking too much 'while I ran'. I enjoy praying and encouraging others while *'on the run'*. These things make *'me who I am'*.

My medical history appears in bits and pieces throughout this book. Even so, I have not included details on all the injuries, operations and years of chiropractic visits, or the times in wheelchairs, back braces and on crutches. Yes, I have put this body through a lot. I know what being *'down'* is like – and how to *'get up'*. I have had years of training on how to '*push forward*'. NOW I will get closer to the '*finish line*' of my thinking for this chapter.

Last week after running the 10 mile *Wooly Worm Woad Wace* at Banner Elk, NC I drove over to Cana, VA. I stayed that night at a fellow runner's house. Ron Collins is the director of Joy Ranch (a home for children), and he was planning to have a number of the children run a 5K race in Galax, VA. Many of these children know me – or about me. They have often held me up in prayer. For many of them this would to be their first race running with me. I was looking forward to this race because I felt it was a course upon which I could run my best ever 5K. During the early hours of the morning, my body was telling me a different story. Walking was the best I could do. So the question became *"What am I to do?"*

In the warm up area for the race, Ron and I prayed. I tried to jog an easy pace to warm up my muscles and get a better idea of what I could (or could not) do. I was at the start line sooner than I really wanted to be. And, with thoughts of pain and pride, I did my best to stand tall as I continued to silently pray. The race began and those young people saw me start the race that I was so looking forward to doing. I was about to set a new record time for a 5K – though not the kind of record that I had planned.

The view from the back of the pack was very hard to bear at first. Pain and thoughts of running for the wrong reason (pride) were heavy upon me. However, I was able to see a reason for being where I was in the pack when I noticed a young boy on the roadside in obvious pain. Within a few quick moments of encouragement, we were running '*side by side*'. He moved on ahead of me and I was truly happy for him. I soon passed a few of the Joy Ranch group and again tried to encourage by being an example, as I ran limping in obvious pain – pain that did not seem to matter as much any more - well, not that much!

Logos of - *Just Do It, NO Excuses, Have Faith,* etc., flashed before my eyes from their t-shirts. They were here today to run and finish! Yes, more than winning a trophy was at stake here for them and for Rick.

Some of the people from the ranch were not typical runners. They were overweight or underweight. Some had health issues including one who struggled to breathe. I found out later that he was blessed with running a better race than he had been able to in a long time. Ron's mom would go on to win in her age division with a combination of running and walking. Ron would win, and yes, beat me as he used to do! I can still hear the kids yell out to me - "Go Rrrrrick – stay in prayer!" as I went by them. Some of the runners from Joy Ranch ran as a team that day. In reality, we were all part of a team in a special way that day.

The words pride, pain and pleasure are not just words anymore. They are '*word trophies*' placed upon a special shelf in my mind that holds these memories, as well as, the memory of questions and answers that this runner had that day. For example, did I use common sense when I chose to run with that injury? The answers to my questions soon became clear. Maybe they would not be clear to all the runners, but they were clear to this Christian runner. Looking into the eyes of these kids from Joy Ranch and listening to their stories of the race made the answer very clear. More than ever before, I was able to run with my heart – not just my feet.

~~~~~~~~~~~~~~~~

It is alright for us to *be proud of our accomplishments and feel that pride* **whether** we run at a slow pace or at a fast pace. Whether we can finish or not finish, and even if the best we can do is walk to the finish line. Even when our performance in the race isn't ideal, the *pleasure,* **along with**

the pain from time to time, allow us to finish many a course with victories that are only within our heart – leaving us rightfully proud of our efforts.

You Would Not Understand Even If...

The truth is solidly this. Even If I shared with you all of the emotional, physical and spiritual details, you would not understand. Not because you are a person who has not lived the life that I have; not because we may differ in our spiritual or religious faith - not for a number of other reasons. You stare and wonder. Questions are asked about me and why I do what I do. You know that I am in my early sixties, have probably had more accidents than anyone else you have ever known or read about - these facts alone have you just shake your head and wonder. Yes, wonder for a brief moment if I was maybe a little crazy. But, you admit that I look normal - in fact, in great shape and have achieved things that few, if any, of the people you know have ever come close to. Still the questions remain unanswered to the point that you really do not understand why and how I can continue doing what I do.

Then, even though I have shared my personal experiences, honest and exciting details, my answers to those questions are not being clearly understood. You witness what I do. I share the emotional and physical reasons for the drive within me. I share about my Christian faith and how it makes me who I am. It comes back to the original question. You still, like so many others who have never been a part of this way of life nor felt the compulsion to continue, see only the pain, plus the cost and the time it all requires. *Even if I wrote down* the facts and explained the feelings that go down deep and are a part of my very soul you *would not understand.* Your questions would only be answered with complete understanding if you had participated, with the same kind of passionate compulsion as I have.

With photo courtesy of Marathonfoto. © 11/27/03
Marathon Atlanta Marathon

I am a marathon runner. You run one marathon, and that
one draws yet another into your plans before you even cross
the finish line. And each year you participate in numerous
marathons across our great country. If you experience that,
you will not have to ask. Because, then, you will understand.
However, then you (like me) will not be able to effectively
explain it to those who are not actively blessed marathoners.
Only the marathoner knows that the secret, the almost sacred
answer does not rest in words – but in the 26.2 miles. Words
never fully expose the mystery. You have to live it out step-
by-step, water station by water station; from start line to
finish line with the finisher's award medal and ribbon placed
around your sweaty neck and the cape of honor draped upon
your shoulders. The truth is solidly this: understanding is
being a marathoner.

BYPFM

*This was a message of thanks
to a local Bible study group
a week after the Galax, VA race.*

Because **Y**ou **P**rayed **F**or **M**e (**BYPFM**), I had both physical and spiritual strength to go to Galax, VA to run a 10K trail race.

BYPFM, I had the opportunity to encourage prayer with a young mother whose faith allowed her to buy herself new sneakers and run the race with her son! The son ran because I was able to buy him new running sneakers and pay his fee for the race. The challenge of *"if you will run I'll pay the fee and buy you new sneakers"* was not quickly accepted. However, since prayers were already at work for the weekend visit – the offer was accepted.

BYPFM, I was able to encourage Director Ron Collins of Joy Ranch Home for Children to ask his adopted son to run with him! Standing tall, side-by-side, they were at another starting line in their life.

BYPFM, Ron and I joined together to say a prayer for this special occasion, and gave thanks for us being able to both run in this race. Fellowship, praise and prayer plus a victory meal was celebrated afterwards; more on that later.

BYPFM, I was able to lift up Ron's spirit. He not only ran, but won in his age group. In fact, it was the best race he'd ever run!

In addition to all of this - the finish line was a time full of excitement with PTLs heard loud and clear. Everyone from the Joy Ranch not only finished in that soaking rain - but also won a trophy in his or her age group. Yes - everyone - even the mother and son! *'Holy Spirit Power'* sent by you *ahead of time*. What about me? I finished 8th overall and won in my age division. In celebration we were led to form a circle and thank God for His Holy Spirit blessings that were 'rained upon us' that special day.

We all went out for breakfast, sat around a large table, placed our trophies upon it, and ate a victory meal. Were we still wet? You bet. The glow coming from the table was not only coming from the trophies – the group was a living testimony to the 'Son of God'.

Back row left to right: ME, Dawn Romasco and
Pastor Ron Collins
Front row left to right:
Michael Collins (Pastor Ron's son) and Kyle
Hodgson (Dawn's son)

Because You Prayed For Me. Five letters beginning five testimonial words are clearly set upon my heart and mind forever. They proclaim the story of a spiritual victory and the power of a *prayer request* at a Bible study.

Shadow Running

I am sure that most of you folks have heard or read about *'shadow boxing'*. No doubt the question you are asking is: "What in the world is Rrrick talking about now and what does that have to do with running? I will be glad to explain. First let's look at the definition of the word *'shadow'*: *a figure projected by the interception of light; shade; an inseparable companion; an imperfect representation; to represent faintly; to follow closely.* This should work nicely to get me were I want to go with my course on 'Shadow Running'. And remember, years from now runners will recall that they first read about it here long before it became popular worldwide!

I have to admit it has a few drawbacks. At night unless you are near good streetlights it does not work well at all. In fact, there is a side effect to it. And – it is evil! I will not scare you off with that now or you will not read on

When I run, I have a lot of fun and I never feel as though I am alone. In fact, I often run with a friend. I enjoy this guy a lot. He is very quiet which allows me to do **'all the talking'**; a lot of runners just can't seem to talk while running – I just do not understand that. Anyway, we worked out a new form of working out: **Shadow Running**. It is very basic. In the next paragraph you will read, understand, and be able to go out and try it yourself.

Why the name? Oh? Did I forget to tell you? My friend is my shadow. If you want, go back and read the definition again. I will wait —- (you back? good!). Well, where was I. Oh, about my friend — I try to not let him pass me. Sometimes he stretches out real wide like a fool and loses a lot of time but I quickly make a turn and he is put back in his place. Sometime I look over my shoulder and he somehow *'drafts off me'* and that bugs me a bit, but as a Christian I need to just let it go. After all, he is a part of me in a way.

Oh, I almost forgot. Do you remember that scary part that I warned you about? Please be very careful when you run at night. That friend of mine has friends who will run with you also. They are not always nice. They will *jump out of nowhere* and scare the living *daylight* out of you! You will trip over your feet, or if I may use the expression, '*Trip over your own shadow*'. Mr. Shadow will pull out ahead of you and you will come to a sudden stop and feel like a fool. I have. Once during a late night run in a quiet area of town it happened and I aged a number of years! My hair is grey enough already and as far as adding years –I'll not go there!

Shadow running – *are you brave enough to try it?*

Too Soon To Quit!

C. S. Lewis wrote, "*God whispers to us in our pleasure, speaks to us in our conscience, but shouts to us in our pain.*" That quote is from his great book *The Problem of Pain* (New York: Macmillan, 1962 – pg. 93 ©). I came across that C.S. Lewis line in a more recent book, also great, by George Sweeting: *Don't Doubt in the Dark* (Moody Press © 2000). The title of this article is part of a quote by William Cameron read as part of a radio script from 1937! The complete quote was *"It's always too soon to quit."*

Now that you have that background information, I will share why it is so important to share it. First, we runners need to be well read. The better read we are - THE MORE EFFICIENT WE WILL BE. Not just in running, but in many areas of life. It goes beyond just the reading of magazines and books about running. Are they needed and enjoyable – yes! However, they are not enough to have you continue improving in all areas of your life.

I can already hear the comments such as *"If I continue with an injury, I'll…";* *"Financially I'm about to go broke and if…";* *"My spouse has had it with my running all these races and…"* – I have already heard and thought about these and more! Let me ask you this: How many times have you wanted to *drop out of a race just because you were not running well or just did not feel like running that day?* The body does not always want to run – especially 26.2 miles! You usually find that out way before the end of the race - I know that I do!

We may be in great shape, well trained and rested up for the event but our mind may not be ready. Fear and doubt sometime override all the preparation. *"It's happened to all of us. There you are, at an event, when it hits you – paralyzing fear and doubt. Your hands start sweating, your heart races and you think, 'I JUST CAN'T DO THIS.' Learning to deal with fear and pushing through resistance is an important skill to overcome obstacles and reach your goals."* That quote is part of an article done for Active.com© by Alison Arnold Ph.D. and James Whittaker Ali entitled 'How to Get the Best of Fear'.

Many a race (goal) is lost in our mind before it is lost on the course. Fear of not being qualified to continue at a set pace has caused me to finish a marathon with left over energy because I had thought myself out of what I could have done. I had 'quit too soon'. My body and mind were not on the same page – they did not agree.

Knowing the definition of words does help. I have blended this knowledge with faith and prayer to help me during these *'testing times'*. Knowing that one of the definitions for fear is *"to stop trying; accept or acknowledge defeat"* (Random House Unabridged Dictionary © 2006) now helps me see what is really at stake when I have fear and doubt. A different view of 'fear' gives me strength and clear thoughts. Random House and the Bible agree: *"Extreme reverence or awe, as toward a Supreme power"* – Psalm 111:10a declares, *"The fear of the Lord is the beginning of wisdom."* Further study in both books will help even more. Yes, reading is physically and spiritually a *win-win* for runners. We need never be in the dark about the battle that is going on in our lives. Yes, there will be pain to brush against the pleasures of the sport, the distance will always be marked out the same, and our training will draw us physically close to a point where we can only do so much. In running and in all areas of life, knowledge, preparation, and faith in God and ourselves will help ensure that we do not quit.

Jacksonville Bank Marathon & 1/2 Marathon
Jacksonville, FL - 12/14/2003

brightroom, Inc.

NEVERTHELESS, *it's always too soon to quit!*

My Achilles Heel

The ancient Greeks told a story of a warrior named Achilles. His mother had been warned that he would die of a wound, so she dipped her infant in the river Styx. That was supposed to make him invincible. However, she held him by the heel, which the protective waters did not cover. It was through that heel that he received his fatal wound.

I am going to share how this old story now has a new meaning!

Drawing by Kourtney Parramore

I read a devotion recently with the title - My Achilles Heel. It really got me thinking. As I am writing this, I am less than two weeks away from running a special marathon at Myrtle Beach, VA. It is special because it will be my 10th different state which will allow me to join both the *50 States Marathon Club* and the *50 States and DC Marathon Group.* However, more than that reason is this – they (the people running the Myrtle Beach Marathon) have written a short piece about me and are putting that plus an article I wrote in the runner's packet. I received a call a few weeks back and was asked a few questions and, well - I now have a chance to share my reasons for running as I do.

My Achilles tendons have been very sore for a number of months. After three years of running with the Salisbury Rowan Runners Club, I am concerned about 'a *problem*' with a running injury. My left Achilles is now fine but the right one is only *okay*. That devotion that I read had me wondering about more than the injury. I realize that in addition to physical problems, Christian runners' have weaknesses in their spiritual armor and that *temptation has many different sized and shaped arrows*.

NEVERTHELESS, some temptations and injuries can make us stronger to serve a *higher purpose*. The fear temptation **not** to run is real. The temptation to prove to myself that I can *go that extra mile* while in pain pulls me forward and allows me to share more of my Christian faith. God has been very good to me and I want others to feel *His power and love*. I may, and probably will, only 'jog and walk' a number of miles in this next race — but I want to be there to talk, pray and listen, and pray with anyone who may have their own story to share.

REMEMBER that *'faith can overcome fear'*. Our **greatest weakness** is often our failure to ask God for *His Strength*. *"I can do all things through Christ who strengthens me."* (Phil. 4:13).

Thinking logically or conservatively would have left me in a wheelchair two times in years past. At Myrtle Beach, I will be prayerfully taking each step as I have done for the past 7,500 miles during these past exciting three years of running. I believe that the *'arrow aimed at ending my running days'* will not hit its spot. This Christian will see the finish line at Myrtle Beach!

On that February day in 2004, I did successfully finish my 10th state marathon. The Achilles heel injury did not strike, but another **situation came up!** The packets did contain my article as part of their runners focus theme: **'Why I Run ...Marathoners Share Their Stories'**. The problem (and embarrassment) was that they had deleted all mention of my divine healings! It appeared that 'I' just got up and ran on my own. The article made me look like some kind of 'super ego hero'. The quote was correct that said - *"You do not know until you try."* They had just left out the part about 'praying' and 'faith'. It was an injury of a different kind for me - not one listed in any running magazine or book.

In addition to the heel problem that day, I ran while on an antibiotic for an ear infection. When the sun came out, well, the last few miles were done at a jog at best. My training for this marathon *and my faith and prayer* got me through the miles and Jesus, once again, strengthened me enough to cross the finish line.

The Fun Runner

The race was about to start and we were about to run head-on into a 35 mph wind. The cool temperature in the low 40s added to the task before us. I made a promise to run along side a man who I had only known for a few months, a man who had polio as a child and still fights the dark shadows of its signature. He was now standing tough and still believing me at my word to keep the promise. We had a five hour running plan for the **2004 Ocean Drive Marathon** in New Jersey. I never ran a marathon at such a slow pace and was concerned with more than just the weather. It was going to be a very long time on the 'point to point' course and a hard promise to keep.

We did just fine for the first few miles. In fact, he even took some pictures of the beach homes and the birds on the beach along the course. Between the laughs that flowed from him, he talked about the kiss he would receive from his wife, Diane, at mile ten. He reminded me that she would take care of our jackets and running pants that we were to stop running and quickly remove. He received the kiss and we kept all of our running gear on! We knew before we reached her that the clothing was staying where it was – no words were exchanged – just expressions of what the situation was becoming.

The waves and mist were almost exciting to see and feel if it were not for the fact that we were already feeling numb from its effect on us. By **mile 11**, we felt beaten by the wind and the sand that seemed to be hitting us without mercy.

Although I noticed that his facial expressions were serious, his voice continued to encourage the many runners that passed us by; not to be overlooked was the fact that he even thanked every police officer along the route and had funny comments for the workers at the water tables.

By midpoint, we were having a hard time even though going at a slow pace. The sand that was blowing at us made it difficult for us to believe that we were on a road at all! It even became too cold for his camera to work. The bridges seemed to reach to the sky; Coast Guard members on them smiled and cheered as we *slowly* passed by them.

The **mile 20 marker** that came into view added another factor to our race. At that point in the race we no longer saw any runners behind or ahead of us. I think that was the last time we talked about how long we had been on the course. The wind was getting even stronger and the waves were splashing over the sea wall on to us. I heard him call out to me asking if I wanted to run ahead; I answered no and just pushed ahead *side by side, step for step with him.*

At **mile marker 21**, I heard him call out the same question that he had asked the many passing runners: *"Having fun still?"* Yes and no I said to myself. His smile encouraged me to say *"Yes."*.

I began to hear his foot drag more loudly now – I was concerned for him. When I asked if he was all right, he smiled and said that he was. The same answer as the other times I had asked him – I was not. My current pace seemed to be more like running in place than moving forward and was hurting my toes that were both cold and burning at the same time. Realizing that he was struggling valiantly, how could I say anything negative to this positive thinking Christian man whose faith towered mine?

The **25-mile marker** was now in view and I asked him if he wanted to run the last 1.2 miles to the finish line. His answer was *"I am running! Let's finish close together for the finish line picture!"*

I agreed knowing that the picture would be one we would look at often as a reminder of this challenging marathon; although it would not clearly reveal what we went through to finish it.

The marathon was over and the clock displayed a clocked time of almost six hours (5:49)! A promise made was kept. His 62nd marathon was completed. And me? Well, it was my 12th marathon completed and my 11th in 13 months. *"Think of it as a PR for New Jersey – not a PW (personal worst) for a marathon."* was his remark when we talked about the finish time over a nice cup of hot coffee.

I am looking forward to doing another marathon with Mr. Freeman Gerow at my side. I want to once again experience his encouragement, jokes, and Christian friendship. I pray that the weather will be kinder for us then!

We did run two more marathons before Freeman passed away after complications from a back operation.

Photos taken by Mrs. Gerow
2004 Ocean Drive Marathon
Cape May County, NJ

The Athens Marathon Experience

As the famous line by Charles Dickens states, *"It was the best of times; it was the worst of times."* Take a moment to read the great opening sentences from *A Tale of Two Cities* before we get back into the winter race in Athens!

"It was the best of times and it was the worst of times, it was the age of wisdom, it was the age of foolishness, it was the epoch of belief, it was the epoch of incredulity, it was the season of Light, it was the season of Darkness, it was the spring of hope, it was the winter of despair, we had everything before us, we had nothing before us, we were all going direct to heaven, we were all going direct the other way - in short, the period was so far like the present period, that some of its noisiest authorities insisted on its being received, for good or for evil, in the superlative degree of comparison only."

The weather was changing from rain to snow to hail faster than I could make up my mind what I should keep on for a jacket. Like Charles Dickens, I felt like I was in a winter of despair – well, at least during these few hours during this marathon in Athens.

The sun showed its face between these elements from time to time to further confuse the decision-making. By the way the weather kept changing - well, I felt that I was back home in the Boston area. However, I clearly knew where I was running this marathon – I was in the city of Athens.

The day started with me awake well before the alarm clock went off. I was very excited about being here to be part of this marathon. Upon looking outside from my motel room and seeing the rain coming down so hard, my heart was pulled to the mood of disappointment because I was hoping for cool dry weather. By the time I got to the starting line area the rain had backed off and the sun was attempting to shine its face. It would be a quick appearance because Mother Nature had a few April Fools Day jokes set for us as we ran on that April 4, 2004 morning. I noticed that there was not a single porta john in sight. Upon asking a few young people standing near me, I found out two facts. First, it was their first marathon and they did not have a clue about such needed things, and they had not seen any in the starting area. Just then, a young woman (early twenties?) made the remark *"Just talking about it caused me to have to go!"* I smiled back at her as she invited me to go to her office that was near by to use the facilities. After a quick jog, we were there and soon back in time for the starting gun to begin our 'Athens Marathon Adventure'. I saw only three porta johns along the course! In addition, with the river off to one side and a steep hill on the other side of the narrow out and back trail course – well, runners were clearly out of luck should they want to hide behind a tree for privacy with their needs.

I had planned to run at a ten minute pace; slow enough to enjoy the course, converse with some runners and not get hurt. At mile twenty, I had plans to eat a few Fig Newton® to help me finish strong. As I pulled them out of my side pack and tried to eat them, they felt a bit strange and tasted a bit dry and crunchy – so I washed them down with a quick sip of water and continued on my way. But wait! What was that pain I wondered? I soon realized that I had just swallowed a tooth (and gold crown). Continuing to run I spit up some blood (gross looking on the snow) and did my best to keep my tongue out of the newly formed hole in my mouth!

The finish line was a welcome sight. The hail had stopped and I was able to run a little faster. Only two laps around the track and this special marathon would be history for me. Upon crossing the finish line and receiving the finisher's medal someone yelled out to me *"Come back here!"* With a quick turn and a few shaky steps in retreat, I was soon smiling while being told that I had won my age division! The special cups were being passed out then (seems like everyone wanted to just get out of that foul weather and get going!). The Grecian Gods, like in the storybooks, were smiling upon me. Well, that thought did pass through my mind.

While driving back home, the snowstorm caused me to be very attentive to my driving. However, I did glance more than once, at the great mock turtleneck long sleeve shirt (with its Grecian style wording), my medal and the neat cup for the division win. My thoughts about the fact that I may never make it to Greece to run in its' marathon were clearly matched with my thanks to my Lord Jesus for allowing me this interesting *'Athens, Ohio'* marathon experience. But who knows for sure? Lord willing, I might someday be sharing the *'Athens, Greece'* marathon experience!

In Faith – Not Fear

Within a two week period I was able to take part in two very different marathons. The first was the *Hatfield – McCoy* in Goody, KY.

You could not meet up with a friendlier group of people! They blessed you from the pasta supper and skits until the time you left for home. I believe that you will never see more stops for water and sports drink in any marathon. Their style of friendship even caused the hills to seem not as high or long – well, almost true!

But we know that all marathons are different. The people organizing and running in it were nice folks, but before I get ahead of myself I want to back up to the *'real starting line'* of the story.

Feeling led to do another marathon real soon, I picked up a copy of the Running Journal magazine and checked out the marathon section. *"Great! There is one only about an hour or so from here and I only need to make a quick call."* The decision was made. I left my name and phone number on voicemail. A man called back the next afternoon and informed me that the deadline was that very day! With the needed web site information, I was quick to print and fill out the registration form, write a check, and get it over to the post office. Upon getting back and looking at the web page again, I read the following (in part, to save space here).

THE MANGUM TRACK CLUB
Live in faith, not fear
Boogie Marathon
(June 2004)

MARATHONERS BEWARE:

This is not your normal marathon. This is all rural, not a city marathon. The course is not certified. You will be in the middle of nowhere all of the time and with no fans, no porta-potties, no miles markers, and no spectators. There are only 6 houses on the course and they have dogs. Aid stations are 5 miles apart so you will need to carry a water bottle. If you decide to quit, there are no pick-up vans, so you will have to stop at the aid station or hitch a ride back to your car. The race will start at 6 pm and the temperature will probably be 85 [was **93!**] *degrees with little light... Think long and hard before you enter this event...the course: short out and back to the start; 10-mile loop (7.8 is state highway; the rest is a state maintained dirt road.)* [Through the **woods!**] *This is not mountainous but is not flat.*

Since faith is an important part of my daily life, I decided to look up the word '**fear**' and read how it could apply to running this marathon: *"...an unpleasant, often strong emotion caused by the anticipation or awareness of danger for alarm / cold feet."*

The word *'faith'* was refreshing to read about after that! Most of us know it to be *"A firm belief in something for which there is no proof or complete trust or confidence in a person, idea, or thing."* I like to read chapter eleven from the book of Hebrews. It is a great chapter about faith. The chapter starts: *"Now faith is being sure of what we hope for and certain of what we do not see."* Christians have proof, God's Word - the Bible, to strengthen their faith. Faith overcomes the darkness of fear. Amen!

Now back to the events of the marathon. Wanting to get in as many miles as I could before it got dark, I ran as fast as I could. The heat was not all that bad after awhile and the hills were just that – hills. However, they did seem to go on forever. The only flat area was the bridge over the creek.

Here is a good laugh for you now! I had decided to *go for it* and not use my flashlight (except to check now and then for the turning point marks on the course). I just closely watched the white line on the highway, and everything was going smoothly. Then, when I looked up again to see if anyone was coming in the other direction I noticed a *bright light right in front of me!* I quickly moved off to the side and as I was doing that, I noticed that it was only a large *firefly!* I felt a little embarrassed. Angels probably even got a good laugh at that show!

At the last checkpoint, I was told that I was in third place. Faith and fear were side by side at that point. I asked myself, *"Third place in a marathon? Yes it was a small group, but these were real runners-* and most of them were a lot younger!" Before long I had to rely on my adventurous faith to lead the way. Yes, I would need to pace myself better in that dark stretch, but as tired as I was – no way was I about to be passed in the dark. It was to be my night to *shine!* Faith is also a *'mental acceptance or actuality of something"* – the truth was set in my heart and mind that I was going to reach that finish line in third place. **And I did!**

A Winner Like Him

Have you ever wanted to be just like one of the great and famous runners that you have seen or read about? Maybe it was someone in your running club or in one of the running clubs in your area? I have for sure! You probably read about this person in one of the running magazines and said to yourself - *I can do that!* You have probably read and studied articles such as: 'How to Run Faster', 'How to Run Longer More Efficiently', 'Three Weeks to a Faster You!' Moreover, the reading did not stop there! More articles were read about how to eat healthier, about sports drinks, new and improved sneakers, strength exercises, running camps, and then you purchased books by the people you want to try to be like. Before long, you were trying different running and exercising workouts. You maybe even thought about investing in a personal trainer to help you achieve your goals. The hours included time at the local health center lifting weights or using the treadmill, elliptical machine, stepper and stationary bike. Maybe you even added bike riding for some cross training (you convinced yourself that the cost of a bike would be well worth it). And how about the time at the Yoga and various exercise classes? Hmm, *am I just sharing the notes from* **my** *logbook and journal?* I think not!

Let us look at the results of all these efforts and expenses. **Yes**, you are healthier (and probably more sore than ever before), and maybe even faster and more confident in yourself. You might also be seeing your name in print for winning your age group for the first time. PRs are now being recorded in your logbook. Looking back, you see that the time and expenses were a good investment. You **did** improve. You may have even come close to or were able to achieve the running times that you thought you were capable of doing.

In the past, the reading of many articles and books has improved and taken me to a higher level of accomplishment in different areas of my life. One such book was '**In His Steps**' - written in 1896 by Charles M. Sheldon. This book is proclaimed the tenth most read book in the world and many believe that its story may have changed more lives than any other outside of the Bible.

*"In simple style, **In His Steps** tells the story of self-satisfied congregants of a Midwestern church who are challenged by a tramp during a Sunday service to live up to their declaration of faith. The tramp then dies in their midst. So moved are the minister and his parishioners that they pledge to live their lives for one year asking themselves, "**What would Jesus do?**" Their example of how they suffered, faced ridicule and emerged victorious inspires other churches throughout the country to do the same."* (**See** article by Chuck Neighbors – "The Story of In His Steps" at Google®).

I have read and applied the information found in running magazines and books to my running efforts. I have studied God's instruction book, the Bible, and have applied the information to my daily life. **The results** have had this *Born Again Christian* witness the *'Good News' of Jesus Christ* across America, while setting PRs and winning numerous trophies and ribbons. *Every* training mile, *every* race and *every* step of *every* day I joyfully do as a witness *'In His Steps"*.

My challenge to you is the same one that I asked of myself: *"Are you willing, by the power of the Holy Spirit, to walk* In His Steps?"

*"To this you were called, because Christ suffered for you, leaving you an example that you should **follow in his steps.**"* (I Peter 2:21) *"...**train yourself** to be godly. For physical*

training is of some value, **but godliness** *has value for all things, holding promise for both the present life and the life to come."* (I Timothy 4:7b-8)

I pray that many of you reading this will be daily mindful of the question - *"What would Jesus do?"* while you press forward with perseverance to show others how to be '*A Winner like Him'.*

Tulsa Oklahoma Marathon 11/19/05
Photographer Karen Thibodeaux
3:50:21

"I fell down and..."

Picture taken by Annie Leazer.

We have heard *"I fell down and I can't get up!"* before. Maybe it was on a commercial a few years ago, or in jokes we have heard with that line in it. Sadly enough those words, or words to that effect, may have come from our own lips at a serious moment in our life.

I had such a moment during the 2005 **Rocket City Marathon**, in Huntsville, AL. At mile marker twenty-five, I was at a pace to maybe do a PR. I was excited at the thought of it and felt strong — so at that marker I increased my pace to get the best time I could. As I went by the twenty-six mile marker I could see the finish line clock and saw that I still might be able to achieve that PR. With an extra effort I pushed forward even faster and... well, my left foot brushed a rock that was projecting out of the uneven pavement and **I fell down and could not get up!** My body was in a strange position and the muscles in my legs were screaming out in pain (the cuts on my left knee and left shoulder were not a fact to me yet). All I could see was a large man looking down at me with an expression of shock.

"Help me please!" was my plea. He continued to just stare at me. After what seemed to be an eternity down on the ground, I was helped up and started moving away from the man (and a woman) who had lifted me up and I was heading, again, toward the finish line. I gave it all that I had left in me - but the clock had beaten me - no PR was to be recorded that day (finished with a 3:42:01). The only new thing recorded was my name and number in the first aid room where I was taken. I had nothing left in me but pain. I should add here that the woman who helped me looked for me later and found me in the eating area sitting at a table. She expressed that she was glad that she could help – BUT never thought that I would be able to ever run off like I did. *"You marathon runners are something else!"* she concluded as she smiled and walked away.

I was fortunate to receive help. It allowed me to get up and complete the marathon. Okay, I did not reach my goal but did have a chance to try at it. Other times in my life I have had other people help me *'when I fell'* into troublesome times such as financial and spiritual problems.

How about you? Can you think back when someone helped you? How about when you were able to help others? Maybe it was even at a race! Whatever the place or reason — only the background for the situation is the fact that is important. Someone gave of themselves to *help someone who had fallen down*, either physically, emotionally, or maybe spiritually.

As a Christian, I am and will be eternally grateful that my Lord came to help me because of my fallen condition. I am now able to be part of and have spiritual inner power to be able to finish the course before me. The time of completion does not matter. What matters is being faithful and steadfast and moving forward.

Let us always be aware that someone may need our help as we pass though the course of life. There is a great celebration awaiting those who *"...run with perseverance the race marked out for us..."* (read Hebrews 12). **No one needs to be 'left behind'.** Prayerfully we will be aware of any need and offer the appropriate support.

With photo courtesy of Marathonfoto © 12/10/05
After I got up and continued to run the final .2 to the
finish line.

Running a Marathon
(While they)
ReCOVER, ReBUILD and ReNEW

I just got back from New Orleans where on 02/05/2006 I took part in their historic *Mardi Gras Marathon* with this year's theme of: **ReCOVER, ReBUILD, ReNEW.** I ran the streets that are still showing signs of Hurricane Katrina's wrath. One could not run through *'The Big Easy'* without recalling the devastating images seen on television. It was impossible for me to not remain in prayer for the city and its people. The water is gone from the city streets but the damage is still clearly visible. As I looked up and saw the water lines two stories high on the homes and businesses, knowing the water came from the breached levees – I could not imagine where the water went. I felt as if I was running through a bad dream that flashed bits and pieces of incomplete news clippings.

This verse was written upon my heart as I ran through the French Quarter:

> *Trees still bow low*
> *Broken in spirit;*
> *Street signs bend over*
> *Defying direction.*

I noticed that many of the faces of the locals seemed to glow with hope, faith, courage and a hardy *'stick-to-it'* determination. They cheered and had the same spirit that we had running the marathon; the spirit needed to finish the course set before us. Enduring their own private marathon through the memories of pain, thirst, hunger and the seemingly endlessness of it all, the finish line *would not* be in sight for them on that marathon day. However, they were already winners in my heart. I saw them as being in the process of shining up their city, which *was their trophy!*

With photo courtesy of Marathonfoto.

3:46:17

Finishing a Beginning

Pictured above the boldly printed title of the article in the Denver Post were five faces representing the many who took part in the Denver Marathon. The writer, John Meyer, must have clearly known what it takes to run a marathon. His title, **FINISHING A BEGINNING**, was a good beginning for his fine article. Additional words above the pictures also shouted the truth: **"Participating is empowering. Training for life and a marathon. Runners conquering challenges."** The shots of the faces silently proclaim that maybe something more personal led each of these people to this moment - but - the writer's titles indeed reflect the truth of just about every runner's experience.

It took something special for each person to start and finish the marathon that day. I would have liked to talk with each of the other runners who were in that picture with me and hear their story – and have the opportunity to encourage them either to stay on the course to Heaven - or to get on it. My prayer is that another Christian runner will have that important conversation at another marathon.

When I look at these facial expressions, I think about seeing similar expressions at the finish line in Heaven. One face may show just how hard it was to get there. Another may show relief at having made the right choices in order to reach this special finish line. But, sadly, some will show pain because they will not **be allowed to cross the line into Heaven.** As Christian runners, we have a responsibility to share the *'Good News'* with our fellow marathoners. It is *a 26.2 mile street ministry* at every marathon.

"Faces light up as runners cross the finish line of the first Denver Marathon." John Meyer shared stories about some of the marathon runners. One woman qualified for the Boston Marathon that day

"…crossing the finish line …with a blissful smile and arms raised in triumph. Today she goes to the doctor to find out how far the cancer that started in her liver has spread."

Some shared these other reasons for running that day: *to achieve emotional growth* after surviving an abusive relationship; *to lose weight; to find strength inwardly to tackle a doctoral thesis* and others ran *to help friends finish* the 26.2 miles. Others, like me, were there to complete another state in my quest to run a marathon in all of the 50 states (and in Washington DC). I also wanted to encourage other Christians to be more open to share their faith while they travel across our country. Moreover, the most important reason of all – to lead others to the knowledge of my best friend – *Jesus Christ.*

Denver Post / Mathew Staver & Lyn Alweis

Those faces represented *another story to me.* You could clearly see that the race was made up of both males and females of different ages and ethical backgrounds. You could even see that marathon runners come in many different sizes! To run all you had to do was sign up and pay the registration fee. All were welcome to be a part of the event.

Not all would finish. Some would finish many hours later and would be seen crossing the finish line running, jogging and yes, some would be seen just walking. The pace did not matter. All that mattered that day was what the title proclaimed: **FINISHING A BEGINNING.**

You can read the emotions on each face. You can see pain in my picture as my lungs were screaming for air! You can see what looks like a combination of exhaustion and the relief that comes from being able to say, *"YES, I Made It!"* You can also see a *silly moment expression.* I wish everyone could be at the finish line of a marathon to observe and be a part of the celebration with someone. Each would be blessed in a special way and feel a part of the day and the victory.

Heaven will be like this. People from **all** walks of life, with many different stories of their journey, and various degrees of pain will cross over the finish line. And, sadly, others will not be there. The ones who *lost faith in themselves or let the pains in life cripple their efforts. Others will never accept the invitation or care about getting across the finish line.*

The Bible *opens* with **"In the beginning...."** and *ends* with our Lord welcoming us across the **finish** line. If you want to begin *(or continue again),* now is the perfect time. The course is still open to you. If you have not signed up, so to speak, I encourage you to do so *(with no registration fee!).* We can continue together with shared encouragement and the joy of victory before us.

Who Moved the Finish Line?

This article came to me because of a book I read a few years ago. The book title comes to mind during many marathons (and sometimes even 5Ks!) because I feel that way about the *'finish line'*! I am sure many of you have read the book by Spencer Johnson titled *Who Moved My Cheese?* ©.

I struggle 'a bit' in races these days. I want to believe that the course is just another difficult one, and I have successfully run many difficult courses before. My body is able to hold up to the challenge, continue to the end with speed, and receive the award for overcoming both the course and many of the others runners. Well, the course and the other runners **are the same**. I, however, am not. Rrrick is getting older.

Since I moved to the Tampa, FL area a few months ago, I have had to deal with different kinds of weather conditions. My seven years in North Carolina were hard enough to get use to compared to my years growing up in Massachusetts. This fact is clear to me – I have to run a little slower with such high temperatures and humidity. But, these facts do not change the mystery about the *finish line* that seems to be moved ahead so often.

As I run, thoughts such as these share the miles with me: *"I do **not** remember the course being so long or the hills so steep; it must be the heat – yes, that must be the reason."* But, in reality, my age factors into each step I take.

*I am now six-two years old. Since I started to compete in April of 2001 I have been able to log over 14,000 miles and my awarded trophies, plaques, ribbons and the articles I have written for various organizations, newspapers and newsletters number over 200. I have been able to run in forty states toward my goal of doing all of the states and DC. My years with the **Salisbury Rowan Runners** were very rewarding in many ways. The club members there played a major role in my being able to run as I did, and I owe them a lot. They helped me to run better and to feel young. However, age does start to win out. Even with such help as theirs and with staying in prayer during training and races. Life's **clock keeps ticking**.*

Miles do seem to be longer and the finish lines a bit further away now. I enjoy running in the Tampa area but the memories of North Carolina seem heavy upon me at times. My running partner and closest running friend is many miles away back in Kannapolis, NC. I also miss the fellowship that was such a part of the event after the races. Those finish lines have been moved far away from me.

Reality is defined as follows: *'Actual being or existence of any thing; truth; fact; in distinction from mere appearance.'* – Noah Webster (1828) / American Dictionary of the English Language©. The years have **not** changed the meaning. What I think, feel or observe also does not change the truth. No one has moved the finish line in those races. I also know and am comforted by the fact that the most important finish line of all will be waiting for me when I finish my race as a Christian – Heaven.

DNF

I am still **chuckling** as I write this. Just last month (Oct. 2006), I wrote an article with the title - Who Moved the Finish Line? Why do I find this humorous you ask? It is because I found out the answer **the hard way**. Instead of the finish line *only seeming further away, it took on a new meaning in my record book*. Out of the thirty-eight marathons in thirty-five different states during the past few years, I have set a new kind of record. Those of you who have run for awhile have already figured out the title of this article. They are three letters that boldly call out an **un**wanted result and are an embarrassment to many – including myself. They are found on many results sheets at the very end – after the slowest times clocked for the race. No reasons are given – just the **DNF** letters, which mean: **D**id **N**ot **F**inish.

When this happens to a runner, the question "Why?" is asked by not only the reader of the stats but also by the runner. The reader may wonder if the person is hurt and if so, how seriously. Even days after the event is over, the runner is wondering what might have caused him or her not to finish and to be listed as DNF. The reasons may never be fully understood so we just try to put it behind us and train for the next race – whether it will be a marathon or a much shorter race. Not finishing a 5K, 8K or a 10K is not a '*happy ending*' for the training and effort on that race day. Nevertheless, the cost is usually just the registration fee. A **DNF** for a marathon is clearly another matter. The states left for me to do are not within driving distance of my home. So, there is the cost of getting to and from the site and the cost of a place to stay and the meals. In addition, we have the ever rising registration fees! Apart from the cost, we cannot overlook the fact that the marathon "not finished' was run so it could be checked off on the '*states to do list*'. I was fortunate that my three letter marathon was only being done for a practice run while I was visiting my family back in the Boston area. My cost was only a registration fee and time: *time to heal from the injury.*

Now, I'll get back to the questions that result from a *not*-finished race. The first question that comes to mind is: "Could I have done something differently to prevent the problem?" In my case the answer would be 'Yes and No'. I might not have pushed my luck by running in that storm and could have run a lot slower. The light that was attached to my hat was a bit useless in that rain and not bright enough to clearly see where I was running. So, I should have practiced using the light BEFORE that nighttime marathon. Now the 'No' answer. I have run in storms and at about the same pace before without problems. **However, this storm** was different and one that deserved a lot more caution than I exercised for it.

Does it really matter so much to not finish? Are there other lessons learned by not being able to finish or by making the decision to 'not go any further'? I believe so.

There was another time during these past few years of running marathons that I had to call upon my *Christian faith* to help me get over an emotional and physical situation. I had flown to Chicago to run the *La Salle Bank Marathon* and developed one of my cluster headaches the night before the race.

The closest I got to the start line was the TV in my motel room. I was then, and still am, a member of **TEAM 413** (www.team413.org) which is a great Christian running group. The motto on the back of the running shirts **boldly reads:** *"I can do all things through Christ who strengthens me."* (Philippians 4:13) This biblical truth has not changed. It does not mean that as a Christian I will run and finish all my races. However, I will be able to keep my head up and remember what is really important. Not getting to a start line or not being able to finish is not as important as how I respond to the situation. The price of not finishing will not be my inner peace or my Christian witness. That was true for Chicago and again for this latest marathon. We must remember that even though running is a wonderful sport, it is just that — a sport.

The only race that is of *real importance* and the *one* that I will never allow myself to be listed as **DNF** is the *one* that I will continue to run with perseverance. That course is clearly marked out and I am pressing on to that final heavenly finish line. By *'His strength'*, I will not grow weary or lose heart.

As I run these **'earthly races'** I will continue to keep all things in the proper perspective and try to help others to remain spiritually encouraged as we move *'Toward the Final Finish Line'*.

A Death Valley Journal

With photo courtesy of Marathonfoto.

"The Valley of Death, Inyo County, California, is the loneliest, the hottest, the most deadly and dangerous spot in the United States . . . It is a pit of horrors – the haunt of all that is grim and ghoulish. Such animal and reptile life as infests this pest-hole is of ghastly shape, rancorous nature, and diabolically ugly. It breeds only noxious and venomous things . . . Its dead do not decompose, but are baked, blistered, and embalmed by the scorching heat through countless ages. It is surely the nearest to a little hell upon earth that the whole wicked world can produce".
(Anonymous reporter for the *New York World*, 1894)

Friday 12/01/2006

With special deals on a roundtrip fare to Las Vegas, a car rental, a night stay at a Motel 6, and that early discounted signup fee – well, the state of California will be checked off my list of states in which to run a marathon.

OK, *maybe* the writer's words above describing the Death Valley area were a bit scary. BUT – I was going to run in December. Last year in Vegas it was 20 degrees at the start line for the marathon there. AND – the t-shirt will be neat to show off! As far as the course – it will be an out AND BACK course; I like the **BACK** part!

Quiet time with our Lord guided my fingers to some comforting words in the Bible, as it so often does. I'm sure you will be able to recall this special one:

"...He helps me do what honors him the most. Even when walking through the dark valley of death I will not be afraid, for you are close beside me, guiding, guiding all the way." (Psalms 23:3c-4 LBV)

With my running gear, traveling maps and marathon information packed in my travel bag all I have to do now is rest. Even with the direct flights, this trip will include a 3 ½ hour drive from the airport in Las Vegas to the start line (2 ½ to Motel 6 and 1 to the race). Then, of course, it would have to be done again in reverse. Add to that a 6-hour wait at the airport prior to the late night return flight, means that I will go about 25 hours before I can get back to bed. Did I mention the *jet lag?*

Sunday 12/03/2006

The Borax Death Valley Marathon is completed. Another state is done – only 11 states to go (and Washington DC). I'll have a few weeks to heal and regain my strength before heading to Phoenix, AZ. "GO WEST YOUNG MAN!" *will again be the call!*

Highlights: Although the area is almost beyond words to describe and everyone should try to visit the area – my best memories are not of the landscape. Of all the marathons run in the past four years, this one blessed me the most because of special people with whom I ran.

Don't get me wrong!!! I've met and still keep in contact with some great guys (and gals) — but being able to run, share testimonies and pray with these guys for the better part of a marathon was a *win – win* marathon day. Finishing medals and trophies can never compare with this prized bonding between runners in the *same quest of miles, time and faith. The runners who took part in this challenge in Death Valley knew that we all had to pull together over the 26.2 miles. This was not the average marathon being run that day.*

The white salt flats brought to mind what many people in other parts of the country were going through with lots of snow and bitter cold temperatures. As I ran in the dry hot temperatures I was blessed, as I just mentioned, with a number of new running friends: Rick, Shane and Vasilios. During the last miles, Rick helped me get beyond my pain *(ended up with a sprained knee)* and finish the course with *another age division win!*

They not only blessed me during the race but again afterwards with fellowship with their wives. Rick even invited me to stay with his family when I go to Phoenix next month! And besides these neat folks, there were others who exchanged e-mails with me and shared some great stories.

~~~~~~~~~~~~~~

Death Valley had 26.2 of its miles blessed with runners who were *very much alive* and *know how to enjoy life.* **It may still look the same to others,** *but I know of a few runners who will remember it very differently deeply within their heart.*

Baker's Dozen

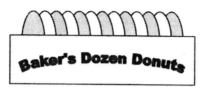

Drawing by Janice Coulter

Many years ago when I worked at Boston's Logan Airport, I often stopped to pick up coffee and donuts for the office team on my way to the office. That was when '*donuts were healthy'!* I can still remember the name of the place because of its name: ***Baker's Dozen©***. They knew what they were doing – a *free* donut **if** you bought a dozen! The extra donut was counted – not the extra calories!

While in Las Vegas for a marathon, I had a chance to view how the *Krispy Kreme Donuts©* people make their donuts. After seeing the donuts floating in oil during the process – well, somehow I missed the point of how that was supposed to cause me to want to eat them and I decided to just have coffee. Time has a way of changing how we see things. Fortunately, our memory of past events and things often allows us to smile in remembrance.

Here is a quick history and trivia for you about the origin of The Baker's Dozen: *"The oldest known source and probable origin for the expression 'baker's dozen' dates back to the 13th century in one of the earliest English statutes, instituted during the reign of Henry III, called the Assize of Bread and Ale. Bakers who were found to have short-changed customers could be liable to severe punishment. To guard against the crude punishment of losing a hand* *to an axe, a baker would give 13 for the price of 12, to be certain of not being known as a cheat. Specifically, the practice of baking 13 items for an intended dozen was to prevent 'short measure', on the basis that one of the 13 could be lost, eaten, burnt or ruined in some way, leaving the baker with the* original *dozen. The practice could be seen in the codes of the Worship Company of Bakers in London."* (Wikipedia ®)

As I am writing this, I can see by the calendar on my desk that a special date (December 12, 2006) is just weeks away. I'm coming up upon a *different* Baker's Dozen. The cost leading up to it has been high and the 13th will not be free – in fact, it will cost me more than any of the others.

My quest to run and to share the gospel and the Christian message in all of the states (plus Washington, DC) will be complete after I run the 13 marathons that remain. The final countdown has begun. One by one and the *'box will be empty'*, so to speak. The last marathon to run will be in Maui, HI (September 16th, 2007). Many miles have been covered with training, racing and prayer since my first marathon in Philadelphia, PA way back in November of 2001.

All of the marathons toward my goal were the standard 26.2 miles; some seemed a lot longer and sometimes were. I did, however, run a *metric* marathon (16.3 miles) up in Wolfeboro, NH back in 2003. By the rules of the marathon clubs - *www.50statesmarathonclub.com* and *www.50anddc marathongroupusa.com* - each race has to be the full 26.2 miles. **Metric does not count** - nor will two halves equal a whole! The measurement is clear and simple.

I feel strongly about my *Christian faith* and consider myself blessed to be able to run all these marathons and able to share the Gospel with as many people as I do on my trips. The Bible has a verse that nicely sums up what I am sharing: *"...if only I may finish the race and complete the task the*

Lord Jesus has given me – the task of testifying to the gospel of God's grace." (Acts 20:24b) Each race flows into the next with the same hope, joy and faith**... I am looking forward** to more challenges after this labor of love is complete. Since the number 3 is a special number in Scripture – well, a *triathlon* sounds **like** a nice challenge to consider!

Press Forward but Do Not Lean

The warmth of the love of our Lord covering me has dried the tears that flowed from my pen while drafting this article and while pouring out the burdens upon my heart in prayer. I still hurt emotionally, but faith in my best friend, Jesus, still sustains me. I will continue in His strength.

As I write this, the calendar shows that it is still a few weeks to Christmas. In 2005, the newspaper article **"They that wait upon the Lord...shall run"** (Salisbury Post© - Faith section / Scott Jenkins) had been published and I was hoping for financial love gifts and for that triathlon bike to show up at my apartment door. Christmas came and went with no bike or financial love gifts. Today the space is clear in our condominium for the bike for which I am still praying. Maybe this will be the year that financial support for my ministry and that triathlon bike will be given and wrapped in His Grace.

The miles are sometimes shared with music from my I-pod, and are always shared with prayers. My heart and mind draw forth the images of people I know and it is almost as if they were actually running beside me. Sometimes people I have not seen or even thought about for a long period of time refresh me with a memory of them. During these miles and this time 'in my prayer closet without walls', nothing else seems to matter....But then I remember -

The financial burden is heavy and my credit card bills clearly prove that. In addition, sadly true, since I started this ministry after my 10th marathon February 24, 2004 – only two couples have sent a 'one time love gift' to help with the expenses. I do not mean to sound judgmental, but if there was a heav-

enly reason for this, I was not aware of it. I clearly did not understand 'the why of it all'.

Clearly and quickly, I mentally see a list of costs to this ministry. It has many areas including that related to my daily pain that calls for meds, doctor and chiropractic visits. It includes the expenses for what is needed to continue doing what this ministry is about – writing supplies, running gear, registration fees, flights, rooms and auto rentals. Next is the invested time for the training, writing, and the traveling to and from the races – and being away from home. The emotional pain with criticism by family members and friends who remind me about my health and finances, and do not offer any help financially is sadly on that list. Then, too, there is the area of relationships/romance – another sacrifice with an emotional cost to this ministry.

For some races, we must travel a distance alone. People who said that they would be there to cheer and help you were not there. Miles would be covered and you might not even know what pace you're running!

Sometimes God has you draw closer to Him to help you take the necessary future steps. He knows best – in that trust we must rest.

The **'pity party time'** did end as I got back into prayer and writing. I saw things more clearly than ever before. The Holy Spirit reminded me that Jesus has paid the ultimate cost at Calvary. Also, I am blessed, not only being 'Born Again', but by being able to share my faith with as many people as I do. Hundreds of people across America are reading about my Christian faith and why I run and share my testimony. Many runners are now more aware of the difference between Christianity and religion — and who Jesus really is. Many, I believe, have been encouraged in their faith.

I need to provide some clarification here about what I mean by the difference between 'Christianity' and 'religion'. Dictionaries define Christianity as a religion. In addition, the majority of people in the world define it as a religion. I go beyond that. When I hear people say *"I am religious"*, and then share that they go to 'such and such church' – but, I do not hear the name Jesus in any part of their conversation – I see **religion only** in their life. I pray that this book will bring to light the difference. The important difference is that one will point to eternity with Jesus on the other side of the final finish line.

My cost is small in comparison to the overall picture of what is at stake. The price of *'the seeds'* that I have been able to sow seems very little now. I realize that I may not see *all of the 'harvest'* until I reach the *final finish line in Heaven* — but each step will bring me closer to that point of celebration. Each pre-ordained step I have run for Christ needs to lead to additional steps to be run in faith. Our Lord, in His Word, tells how that is to be done. Whatever translation read admonishes us to do it *"with perseverance – with patience – steadily – with resolution"* or clearly *"with determination"*. I like how the NIKE® commercial said it - *"Just do it®!"*

By faith, I know that I will continue to *'press forward'*. The only **'leaning'** I will do will be toward the course before me. The members of my family and many of my friends may not recognize the results of my witnessing for Christ until much later down the road – maybe not until they reach the other side of the **'Final Finish Line'**.

SCRIPTURE that is music for the soul!

"I press on toward the goal to win the prize for which God has called me heavenward in Christ Jesus." (Phil. 3:14)

*"Trust in the Lord with all of your heart and **lean not** on your own understanding."* (Prov. 3:5)

"Listen for God's voice in everything that you do, everywhere you go; he's the one who will keep you on track." (Prov. 3:6 MES)

"Don't assume that you know it all. Run to God! Run from evil!" (Prov. 3:7 MES)

I Am NOW Called a Maniac

In my 62 years, I've been called a number of names. Some of them lifted me up – others fell into the *'sticks and stones may break my bones, but names will never hurt me'* arena. I am still not sure if I truly believe that saying, but it gave me something to say back at the kids in grade school. Most of those kids I have forgotten as well as the names hurled at me.

When I took up competitive running again back in 2001 after having not competed since prep school, nicknames appeared again. I received complimentary ones as well as the destructive type because of how many miles and races I was doing. A quick example: I joined the 1000-mile club with the **S**alisbury **R**owan **R**unners club. How was I to know that no one had ever gone over 2,000 miles in a year! I put in over 3,000 miles that first year with the club – and, ran a race every weekend with wins in my age division most of the time. I felt young again and was hooked on running!

I know of at least one person in the club who accused me of not being truthful about the number of training miles I was doing. Many said that I did *too much cross training* at the YMCA. They could not understand why I ran on the *treadmill for hours at a time*, worked *out on the elliptical machine* and THEN headed to the pool to do some *jogging in the water*.

The results of all the hard and timely training were more than just getting into shape and being able to win *trophies*. I was able to fight off the osteoarthritis that was coming on fast and hard in my body; a disease that put me on disability when it caused me to lose the full use of my hands. However, there was a more important reason behind my efforts. Yes! I like winning. However, it is not only for the sake of winning that I still push so hard. It opens up opportunities to share my Christian faith. My testimony, with stories of how doctors told me twice that I may never walk again without difficulty, is always exciting to share!

Bottom line - I stayed in shape and as of this date, I have won numerous trophies, ribbons and plaques and have completed marathons in all 50 states plus DC.

Articles and pictures of me have been in newspapers and newsletters. I have been able to write numerous articles about running and about my faith. Scott Jenkins, from the Salisbury Post©, did a neat story with pictures of me working out in the pool and running. The **bold print** title clearly called it as it is in my life: *"They that wait upon the Lord...shall run"*. That is from Isaiah 40:29-31. The article captured *why* I run and share my faith with that same energy.

You can now call me a MANIAC and I will not take offense. I proudly run with the club's bright yellow singlet with the bold black printing declaring that I am part of the Marathon Maniacs club!

In closing, I want to share two more words that I am proud to say describe me. They originate from a singer - Carmen (www.Carmen.org) and a concert he did by the same title. He asked the crowd if anyone was **Radically Saved:** I answered **'YES!** I am **not** ashamed of my enthusiastic approach to running and to the sharing of my Christian faith. It makes me who I am. I am proud to be a Born Again Christian runner who openly shares the joy and desire of both my faith and this great sport.

Joe Tompkins and Rrrick after the Coeur d'Alene
Marathon
May 2007

Photos taken by Steven Yee - Marathon Maniac #1

This Rush I Have

What do you think about while you train? As you jog, run or maybe walk – during the movement of your feet, where are your thoughts?

When you invest time at the YMCA, or at a health center – while there, does your mind get a workout or does it (how can I politely say this?) just drift and do its own thing while waiting for you to get back to reality?

I have shared with many people that I consider my *'running prayer closet'* to be a lot like the country in the Narnia story by C.S. Lewis. *"What does that have to do with your training?"* you may be asking – I reply *"A lot"*. To me, my prayer closet is like that Narnia closet, which leads into a seemingly endless land. In reality, mine starts and ends at the door of my condominium, and is as wide as my training loop is that particular day. While in prayer, I often forget that I am even running! I feel as if I am flying over the area and spreading seeds of the gospel upon each home I pass. The miles are covered with prayers for the many people who are in my heart - by name. Often I feel led to extend my run because additional people enter into my thoughts that should have a blessing of prayers.

When you are out the door with your headset in place with your favorite music flowing from your I-Pod® and you have your fluids and maybe a few gels – what are your thoughts?

Are you thinking about your pace, the next race, bills, family problems, your job, or what you should (or would rather) be doing?

I eagerly look forward to my time away from my condominium. Don't get me wrong – it's very nice there! However, I feel free being away from the pull of the TV, home improvement projects, house chores, books to finish reading, studies to be done, e-mails to be written, articles to be worked on, and the phone calls to make (OK – I do carry my cell phone BUT, only for an emergency). Is my list about the same as yours?

Aside from all of the items on that list, the most important reasons that I look forward to this time *(which is refreshingly new as each day is)* are these! I have the freedom to pray, listen closely to the words of the songs, and think about what I am in the process of writing for my current book.

Just today, around mile six, I clearly remember saying to our Lord – *"Every day for the past few weeks You have given me an idea for an article – where is it today?"*

Within a few steps, I had not one, but three titles for articles. During the next mile, I knew what each would be about. The titles He put in my head will be – 'M & Ms and...', 'Forgiveness – Going the Extra Mile', and 'Soul Movement'.

I stepped up my pace and felt that I couldn't get to my desk fast enough to write! Once home, it was a PR for my shower time!

Unless you know the voice of the Lord, you may not fully understand this truth as I do. *A runner's adrenaline is wonderful* – but nothing compares to **'this Holy Spirit rush'**.

FOOT-note:

After I finished this paper, I felt led to pray and I want to share that prayer with you.

Thank You, Lord Jesus, for being my training partner. Thanks for guiding me in prayer and giving me something to take back to share with others, again today. Thanks for exercising both my body and mind for Your glory and continuing my running ministry. Amen.

brightroom, Inc.
The New Denver Marathon 2006 - 3:58:42

Forgiveness: Going the Extra Mile

Forgiveness - we all have to deal with it in our lifetime. From the lips of lovers, friends and married couples we hear — "I'm sorry, please forgive me". It is not *just a 'Christian' teaching* although I believe most of us have learned about it through church teachings. Mr. Webster states, in part: *"...signifies toward or back...give...to treat as not guilty."* Sometimes we need to take one step back in order to be able to move forward. In another dictionary the word *'forgive'* is defined: *"To excuse for a fault or offense. To stop feeling anger for or resentment against."* Enough of the quick English lesson and on to the *'running lesson'!*

Race directors have to deal with club members who do not show up to help at a race. Runners often have to deal with 'incomplete kits' (where are the pins!); wrong turns because someone was missing at the corner to point the correct way; late starts; no drinks on the course or not enough drinks and food at the finish line area; presentation not done at time scheduled; wrong race times; and awards given to the wrong people. All of these things have to be forgiven. And, runners have to forgive other runners when they step on our heels, bump us, or cut us off on corners – *need I add more?*

Any of the above can drain us and pull us away from the joy of the sport. And sadly, all too often, cause a problem between club members and visiting runners.

I have had to deal with forgiveness at times as a runner. Typically, the source of irritation was not a big deal and was quickly forgotten. HOWEVER – sometimes it ate at me and drained me of my positive energy and joy. My miles seemed longer and harder. I was guilty of making *mountains out of mole hills*, as the saying goes. The emotional upheaval resulting from not forgiving was a waste of time and energy – worse than doing 'junk miles' for training. As a Christian I knew better but still failed.

People are just that – people. They will forget or just not show up to help. The rules of the road will be ignored. Even such things as the birthday, anniversary or another special event of club members will be forgotten or ignored.

Do we stop running, asking for help at events, trying to be more aware of others during races or e-mailing our friends to share concerns and encouragement? **No!**

Runners are special people who 'go that extra mile' and learn to overcome these mistakes. We look ahead to the open roads and finish lines to be crossed. Our training has taught us well. We know that there is no need to carry extra weight, which includes not forgiving others or waiting to be forgiven. Let's continue to remember this as part of our wonderful sport and draw others to it!

Soul Movement

*The voice deep within my heart softly nudged me to
volunteer at the upcoming Expo.*
I said no.
*The voice reminded me that I should reach out to
the running club members.*
I said that I was not liked; felt despised.
*The voice reminded me that I joined to be a
Christian witness.*
I said it was a waste of time.
*The voice whispered that the club's expo
booth needed help.*
I pouted.
The voice, louder now, said I needed to be there.
I gave excuses that I was running a 15K Saturday
and a marathon Sunday.
*The voice with a heart-wrenching plea said
"Please."*
I stood mentally and physically motionless.
The voice - became silent.

I then saw the angry crowd, a bleeding man,
the cross and ...
became silent as I prepared to obey.

Friday started with problems. I got up late and was
tired because of little sleep during the night; felt restless, was
concerned about the events of the Gasparilla Expo, and felt
uneasy about being in the Tampa Bay Runner's club booth,
as I had never worked one before. I got a late start, missed a
cut off, and could not find a place to park. When I did locate
one, I did not have enough money with me to pay for it. I
had to search again for a cheaper one. After driving around
seemingly forever, I located a place that I could afford.

Another 'Cash Only' – what is the world coming to! I placed the money in the slot, wrote down where the car was located, and then went searching for the convention center. I had to ask someone. Some men DO ask directions! **No one was at the club booth yet. I was alone for the first hour or so – then I was alone, again.** A few volunteers came, worked a few hours and left. My replacement did not show up and I had to stay. I was hungry, broke, tired and wondering just why I was supposed to be there. What good was I doing? I felt that I was representing a running club that did not seem to want me in it. I quietly lifted my broken spirited voice *"Oh Lord! Please make sense of all of this mess"*.

People *walked by and by and by* **– few stopped.** To the ones that did momentarily pause to look, I gave flyers regarding the club's upcoming Strawberry race. Then, I was touched with an idea. I would pray for the people walking by and to the ones that briefly stopped I would offer the card that I have mentioned before in another chapter. I call it 'God's business card' (because God does mean business – He invested His Son's life in it!). This particular card has a small picture of me running, as well as my e-mail address, blog info, and on the back my home address. Yes, I finally understood a lot better now and I felt excited about the *Divine appointment* to be there at that expo booth.

A teenager, very tall and thin, walked up with who appeared to be his father. After answering a few running club questions, I gave him one of my cards. He showed it to his father who gave me *a smile to beat all smiles* – best I had ever seen! I felt a peace that would cover me the rest of the day.

I passed out countless cards, and yes – club flyers. Booth help showed up by mid-afternoon. The next few hours seemed to fly by and then it was time for me to leave. I was quick to leave the expo and head back home – content and anxious to share the day with some close friends by way of e-mail.

I know how blessed I am to be able to reach people like that teenage boy, Chad, who chose to run the 15K. During the following weeks, he and I exchanged numerous emails. He wrote about how he was praying more. Chad also shared how he was putting scriptures on his bedpost to remind him of his spiritual obligation as a Christian runner at his high school. He thanked me for *'encouraging him in the faith'*. As I write this, recent e-mails from him are still blessing me with his great Christian witnessing spirit.

The expo ended up not being the story. Neither was it the 15K race I ran with my chiropractor friend, Scott Paton. It wasn't even the opportunity to help the boys in the wheelchair division of the race. The '2007 Bank of America Marathon' was not the story either! All of this was just like working in the booth – a foundation; a start of what I dare to call *a Christian love story*. **One** that Jesus wrote years ago on a cross. It is the same **One** of which we are all a part as we continue in fellowship along the course before us.

This weekend was a gift from my friend Jesus, one that I will remember and share as a perfect example of *Soul Movement*. I trust that many others like Chad will run races and be strengthened in their faith. Actually, I trust that the 'soles' under those running souls that weekend are one-*step closer* to the most important finish line of all!

Chad Gruber is the runner on the right.
With photo courtesy of Marathonfoto.

The Challenges

The challenges in Tampa Bay during the **2007 Bank of America Gasparilla Distance Classic** were not the distances of the marathon or half-marathon, nor were they the distance of the 15K or 5K race. The challenges centered, within the thousands of runners and spectators, on a little known part of the weekend during the 15K race: **"The Joey Challenge"**.

The two young boys (Joey Chiavaroli and Jerry Lauer) took on the 15K distance *in wheelchairs*. Along with Holly Tripp, who was also involved with the *Joey Challenge*, I tried to get a fast start (the wheelchairs had an earlier start time) to catch up to them to help them up the hill right before the bridge; but no need. These two boys were up and beyond it before we hit that mark.

Dr. Scott Paton of Paton Chiropractic and Sports Medicine and I were running at the newly adjusted pace we'd planned for the day. The reason for this adjusted and slower pace? Well, *another challenge* was in place. A few days before the scheduled 15K event, Dr. Paton hurt his ankle. He asked me to run with him at a pace that would allow us to complete the distance and still have enough time to go back and help the boys complete the distance. Our racing time was but a sidebar of the day's challenge event - we would be but shadows compared to the two courageous boys pushing their way over the course.

I was happy, well – a little, to run at a slower pace because I was also signed up to run the marathon the next morning - *another challenge!* To pull ahead of the story – yes, I was able to run and finish the next day's marathon.

With a fair time (Scott's best yet), we were able to collect our finisher's medals and get back out on the course to help Jerry finish his final mile to the finish line. Joey was already across the line and eager to see Jerry's face at the finish.

"He gives strength to the weary and increases the power of the weak." (Isaiah 40:23)

About Joey's Challenge (www.thejoeychallenge. org):

It was founded in 2005 by a small group of people who wanted to make a difference in the lives of children that are physically handicapped. The organization is an annual wheelchair racing event that is held in Tampa during the Gasparilla Distance Classic. The organization's goal is to provide sports equipment (such as racing wheel chairs and prosthetic limbs, etc.) to children with physical and financial limitations. There are thousands of Joeys waiting for someone to step up and give them the help they need.

Joey Chiavaroli was born in 1995 with Spinal Bifida, a disease resulting in severe damage to the spine and nervous system. Joey also has hydrocephalus, which is an accumulation of cerebrospinal fluid in the ventricles of the brain, leading to their enlargement and swelling.

At the post race celebration, Joey announced that *next year* he is going to enter the half marathon. He said, *"OK – Now I have made it official so I have to do it!"* Everyone laughed and clapped their hands knowing that he would be true to his word.

What about you? Since you accepted Jesus as your Lord and Savior, became a Christian, and made the statement of faith - have you continued to look ahead toward *the final finish line* with the same conviction? I pray that you will be like Joey and know deep down inside of you that the words -

"I have to do it!" - are more than a challenge. They represent a commitment.

After Scott and I finished the 15K,
we went back to find and encourage Jerry
for the last part of the race.
With photo courtesy of Marathonfoto. 2007

Promises and Miles

Each of us has at one time or another made a promise or has had one made to us. There is no deep or hidden meaning to the word. Most dictionaries agree it means – *'To assure one by a binding declaration; hope or expectations; to be assured or have strong confidence.* What I will talk about in this article is the promise one makes to oneself. As for the *'miles'*, our logbooks and body clearly have that knowledge! The logbook entries can be extensive and include things like the weather conditions during a particular run, the kind of workout accomplished during a run, and what was done at the health club or YMCA. Prayerfully, our bodies will show physical progress.

I grew up in Haverhill, Massachusetts. Many famous people have a link to Haverhill. I will mention a few you are likely to know. It is where Rowland Macy opened his first Macy's Department store; Louis B. Mayer of MGM opened his first movie theater; John Greenleaf Whittier found his love of poetry and worked as the local newspaper editor; Bob Montana found inspiration for some of the characters in his **Archie Comics;** and perhaps while Robert Frost was here he found inspiration in our winter wonderland for his poem - **Stopping by Woods on a Snowy Evening.**

That Robert Frost poem came to mind many times when I ran in the woods as a teenager. I thought about the lines that spoke about stopping and observing the area *"between the woods and frozen lake"* and that part about the horse – *"My little horse must think it queer to stop without a farmhouse near..."* And the closing lines are still fresh in my memory:

> *"The woods are lovely, dark and deep,*
> *But I have promises to keep,*
> *And miles to go before I sleep,*
> *And miles to go before I sleep."*

For me, the horse symbolizes my conscience questioning my motives – and perhaps finding them a bit queer. Like the man in this poem, I was dealing with issues in life. His dedication to promises remains strong in his mind. I believe the poet, like the man in the story, knew there were *"promises to keep and miles to go..."* in his own life.

I have mentioned my history of accidents a few times in the previous chapters. The motor scooter accident right after graduation from high school was the beginning of many hospital stays and a lot of physical therapy. Many, including me, thought that my running days were over - well, it would be close to 37 years of additional accidents and recovery time before I was free from the shadow of those health problems. I was not able to run for any meaningful period of time – truthfully, it was more like a jogging pace – during those years. Death was often in my path and called to me to 'just give up'.

But I made a promise to myself in that hospital bed back in 1964. I was determined to not only walk again – but also to run. I trusted God to help me with this promise. He did, in His perfect time. Little did I know that God had a plan and it involved years of training not found in training books. The years of recovering with physical therapy to work through the pain strengthened my character.

"...now that suffering produces perseverance; perseverance, character; and character, hope. And hope does not disappoint us, because God has poured out his love into our hearts by the Holy Spirit, whom he has given us." (Romans 5:3b-5)

My wavering hope during all those years grew to be unquestioned hope – but, only in His time. God's plan that I run for Him was on His perfect timetable. Another Robert Frost poem, **The Road Not Taken,** made an impact on me as a youth. I will share the closing lines from it.

> *"Two roads diverged in a wood, and I –*
> *I took the one less traveled by,*
> *and that has made all the difference."*

I became a Christian in 1974. With that commitment to Christ, I became empowered by the Holy Spirit. I moved forward with a newly enriched faith. I began with jogging. I shared my faith and my testimony, which helped me move forward. But soon health problems crossed my path followed by another serious accident. When told that I might not walk again, I held tighter to my promise. *I knew - that I knew - that I knew,* that my Lord Jesus had a plan for me; I only had to press forward and be faithful.

I have logged over 14,000 miles since 2001 which is when I joined a running club in Salisbury, NC (Salisbury **R**owan **R**unners). I have run marathons (and witnessed) in 49 different states and DC and have scheduled the last state for later this year (September 2007). On display in my home are many trophies, ribbons, plaques and newspaper articles about my running and ministry declaring the *fruits of His blessings* when we trust Him and lift Him up!

Promises to keep and miles to go before I sleep – Yes, this young man of 62 still has many miles to cover, many people to witness to about the Good News, and many Christian runners to encourage who are also taking the less traveled road in this world.

Photo by Al's Studio of Marion ©
Swan Lake Marathon 2007
Swan Lake Christian Camp – Viborg, SD
Tom Detoret on the left
This marathon I wore the **Christian Runners org. singlet**

The Altitude Attitude

Reflecting back, I realize that it could have been just another marathon. However, it was not - it was special, not because it was the 49th different state in my quest to run a marathon in all 50 states plus DC, but for reasons that flowed from God's own hand. In my heart, I knew that I should feel closer to God in these mountains which were a masterpiece among His glorious creations. I struggled spiritually as I ran in these mountains. This was a marathon that came to be blessed by a young Christian man, Phillip Griffith, who showed his unselfish spirit by passing up his chance at a good racing time to stay by my side offering encouragement I needed in order to stay the course. Yes, I will remember those hours on that course for a long time – a course that taught me lessons about the most important course, the course to the final finish line in Heaven.

I was physically standing closer to you, Father God, than I have ever been before. Surrounded by Your tapestry of nature that may have looked as a silent flow of colorful rock formations, I heard music of praise, glory and honor for You all around me. The altitude clearly affected my ability to breathe – but feeling Your presence in a special way humbled me and made me appreciate every breath I took. I remembered the times you spared my life – yes, my every breath surely is a gift from You.

It is easy to look back and see the 'what and why' of a situation. It seems that at the age of 62, I still have a lot to learn spiritually and about life itself! Even the marathons can never be taken for granted, as each has its uniqueness. Let me take you back to the beginning, just yards from the start

115

line, to paint a picture with words about what was happening that day.

Although the running gear I chose for that day was the right choice to help me in my effort, it did not help the effort in terms of spiritual armor.

> *"And that about wraps it up. God is strong, and he wants you strong. So take everything the Master has set out for you, well-made weapons of the best materials. And put them to use so you will be able to stand up to everything the Devil throws your way. This is no afternoon athletic contest that we'll walk away from and forget about in a couple of hours. This is for keeps, a life-or-death fight to the finish against the Devil and all his angels.*
>
> *Be prepared. You're up against far more than you can handle on your own. Take all the help you can get, every weapon God has issued, so that when it's all over but the shouting you'll still be on your feet. Truth, righteousness, peace, faith, and salvation are more than words. Learn how to apply them. You'll need them throughout your life. God's Word is an indispensable weapon. In the same way, prayer is essential in this ongoing warfare. Pray hard and long. Pray for your brothers and sisters. Keep your eyes open. Keep each other's spirits up so that no one falls behind or drops out."* (Ephesians 6:10-18 MSG)

My spiritual strength seemed to disappear just yards into the marathon. Here I was with all this grandeur around me as I began the "2007 Run with the Wild Horses' marathon in the upper desert plains of the Green River, WY. Yet, I had a problem. I very quickly knew that I might as well ignore the pace chart on my wrist for there would be no 3:45

marathon today. I was already in pain – my chest felt like it was about to explode! The altitude was higher at the start of this race than it would be at the finish line. I was told the course would range from 6,200 feet up to 7,600. I thought the 'mile high' course I ran in Denver was tough, but Green River was now at the top of my stress list. Depression was dragging me down. I felt as if my prayers were a waste of time and that I was very much on my own. I was in no mood to witness about the 'Good News'. Who would listen to me today anyway? Even I didn't like being with me! Oh, how I wished that I had picked a marathon somewhere else in this state.

My running watch showed that I had gone less than a half mile yet I was feeling like I had run many miles. *"Where is the first water stop anyway?"*

Although the first water stop seemed very far off, my Garmin® showed that it was right on target at mile one. Within a few quick moments, I felt fine! With a quick drink of water, I was ready to overlook that first mysterious mile and get back to running the marathon.

AGAIN! The pain is back and I have only run a few yards – *"Lord help me!"* was my heart and body's cry. As always, my prayer was heard and answered.

Phil called out to me and soon shared as he joined me 'jogging' that he remembered me from the Swan Lake Marathon in Viborg, SD. He commented how I was an encouragement to him and he was grateful I shared my Christian testimony and encouraged him along that course. *"Don't feel bad about how you feel. This course's altitude is very tough. I will stay and encourage YOU this time!"* True to his word, he did just that all the way to the finish line, where his lovely wife was waiting to take our picture crossing together side by side.

I almost forgot to tell you about the neat age group award I received. It was a real horseshoe spray painted gold! It is a great memento. This marathon was definitely worth doing – even with the new experience of pain in my lungs and the tough spiritual lesson I had to learn. *Yes – it was worth every mile of it.*

This picture is from a Green River Chamber of Commerce Flyer.
We were running – well, jogging high off to the upper right of the picture.
Crossing the bridge with the finish line in view was exciting and encouraging.

More than these...

'**If**' is a word that is like a bridge that connects verbally, but never allows one to get beyond the dream or briefly spoken wishful thought. We have been taught that the word 'if' often indicates a possibility, condition or stipulation. Gathering all of this information, I see it as *more than these* ideas. Look at the word more as *a door of opportunity* – a situation where you can make the decision to change events concerning your life physically, socially and spiritually.

I could *take this time to share about all the wonderful places where I have run marathons across America.* The places would run the gamut of demographic extremes. Courses run below sea level, such as Death Valley which is almost 300 feet below sea level and the lowest point in the Western Hemisphere - and all the way up to heights with altitudes requiring that jogging replace running, such as at the Green River, WY high desert plains area. However, there are *more than these* examples to describe what runners see at these marathons.

There was the marathon with high winds and hail which had the best of runners stop on the course to fight off Mother Nature's nasty side. The marathoners were often dangerously close to being swept off the mountain road to sure death below. Then there was the marathon where runners faced temperatures in the high 90s before they even took their first step. In addition, there were all too many marathons during which the rain was coming down so hard we felt as if we were running upstream; I could have sworn that we passed fish heading downstream more than once. And yet, *more than these* weather related events have been a part of my marathon career.

Not to be overlooked are the times when I saw runners of all ages collapse before me, and others laying on the side of the street obviously in great pain. There were the out and back courses where I'd see a runner heading toward me running faster than his feet would allow causing him to crash face down with blood red becoming the trophy color of the day. The quiet streets did not always conceal the outburst of a painful cry or the sounds of runners gasping for air. I could tell you *more than these* stories that seldom make it to the morning papers. If I only shared some details, I would not be explaining the whole experience. There is a lot *more than these* details that make up marathon events.

brightroom, Inc. © 2007

The apostle Paul often compares running to the Christian experience. We read about the excitement the apostles often felt sharing the 'Good News' with its many blessings promised by Jesus for His followers. However, Paul writes about *more than these* facts. He does not neglect to bring in the details that go from one extreme to the other. Paul shares about the 'Joy' of being a Christian, but also warns about the suffering that we will endure. He writes about the *'high and lows'* - those peaks and valleys that our emotions will go through. He clearly writes that we must be aware of our surroundings; that we are in a spiritual battle and **not** everyone around us will make it to the finish line.

If I lined up the trophies, ribbons and plaques I have been awarded along with the clippings of the articles done about me over the past few years, it would be an impressive display. I am still amazed at what our Lord has allowed me to accomplish during my 'senior' years *(I am being called the Peter Pan Man by a few friends)*. The pictures taken of me running along the different courses and crossing the finish lines have me stare in wonder at how I could smile as often as has been captured by the lens of the camera! Yes, some of the expressions on my face expose the pain I felt, but these pictures do not as easily reveal the joy within my heart – joy that has never been taken away no matter the difficulties of any marathon. I know the whole story. It is *more than these* awards and photos. It has been more than running a marathon in all of the states. It has been the opportunity to share the 'Good News' every place my feet touched during each trip. Symbolically, the Christian fish on my shirt was checked off **before** any of the states on the list. Marathons became my *street ministry*, one mile at a time.

I made a decision back in the 70s to become a Christian. The course that lay before me has been becoming clearer as I studied Scriptures and drew closer to the One Who called me. Each symbolic step was taken in faith. Sometimes I felt as if I was running toward the finish line with all the energy and time I would need to cross it, be with Jesus forever, and have Him say, "Well done my faithful servant." However, I have to confess that all too often there were *more than these* moments in my Christian life. I all too often tripped and crawled in sin. The pain of my disobedience and the conditions that surrounded me were my own sinful fault.

I point each of you *to the final finish line.* Whatever it takes to cast aside worldly things and whenever the sidelines seem to draw you away from the course and steal precious time away from fellowship with other Christians and our Lord, dig deep within yourself and draw strength from the Holy Spirit. He will give you victory at Heaven's glorious finish line!

M & M's® and ....

M and Ms and then more **Ms** – and like the tasty candy with its many different colors, I see the many different marathons that I run. The varying colors of the candy have us anticipating something different, but it is consistently the same - both in taste and enjoyment. The marathons appear to be different, but no matter which city the course was laid out in, it always ends up being the same **26.2** miles. *Marathons and marathons and then more marathons* appear on my schedule each year. And, as a year nears its end, each marathon seems a little more special and more important – like getting to the end of the candies in the bag. One by one the marathons are behind you and then it is time to begin again; not unlike the urge to purchase the next bag of M & Ms®.

Drawing by Kourtney Parramore

OK! I may be making what seems like a silly comparison but please bear with me and *dig a little deeper* to find what I am trying to offer you.

Do you take it for granted that there will be another marathon for you? Does it ever enter your mind that there won't be enough money to register, purchase flights, pay for a room, and rent a car and all of the other things that are needed? Or, have you considered that you won't be well enough or strong enough for the next race? Simple things in life, like being able to have a bag of those delightful little candies, are often taken for granted.

While putting my notes together for this article, I remembered one marathon day when I went into a store to purchase a few snacks for my trip back home. They did not accept the only credit card I had – *it was as if I had no money at all*. I had to leave without any snacks.

Marathons can be like that – sometimes our wallets and our bodies will not be able to come up with what it takes to invest in or complete the race. Because I had used that credit card a number of times during that long trip, the bank did a *'safety stop check'*; sometimes our brain does the same thing. We end up having to leave (that part of our life) without the treat so dear to our heart.

I run for Jesus with my ministry called 'Running Across America'. As of September (2007), I have completed a marathon in all fifty states plus DC. I am now on the path to witness at and run all of the marathons in Florida. I know that someday down the road I will have to cross that final finish line in Heaven. I'm at peace because I know that I am saved and I am confident that I will cross that line into eternity with Jesus. **My questions are – "Are you Born Again? (John 3:5-8) - and just how sure are you?"**

Quite often people ask me how I train in order to be so successful running so many marathons at my age. My answer is that I always start upon my knees in prayer. I suggest the same to them. *"Physical training is of some value, but godliness has value for all things, holding promise for both the present life and the life to come."* (1 Tim. 4:8) I also like the way it reads in The Message© translation: *"Exercise daily in God – no spiritual flabbiness, please! Workouts in the gymnasium are useful, but a disciplined life in God is far more so, making you fit both today and forever. You can count on it. Take heart."* I have never run a race without having prayer as a part of every mile.

Today is the day to highlight your spiritual calendar if you have never accepted Jesus into your life - *"...now is the accepted time; behold, now is the day of salvation."* (2 Cor. 6:2b KJV). If you want to be assured that you will not ever run (pun intended!) out of what really matters the most, make sure that you begin your 'walk' with your Lord and Savior today. Psalm 89:15 states that - *"Blessed are those who have learned to acclaim you, who walk in the light of your presence, O Lord."*

The next time you see a package of M & M's® say a quick prayer thanking Jesus for the mmmmmmmmmmmany blessings that you enjoy now and will for all eternity!

"Taste and see that the Lord is good..."
(Psalms 35:8b)
"How sweet are your words to my taste, sweeter than honey to my mouth!" (Psalms 119:103)

After The Acceptance

You accept the challenge to become a runner.
You read material and ask questions of runners.
You 'step out in faith', train, and put in the miles.

Then the day arrives and you are at the start line to begin the official journey toward being recognized as a runner.

The course will test your training, your physical endurance, and your dedication to continue to the end.

~~~~~~~~~~~~~~~~~

You accept the challenge to stop living as a sinner, as one who does not have a personal relationship with God, does not know Jesus as Lord and Savior, and does not recognize the power of the Holy Spirit. So now, you want to become a Christian.

You read some Christian material and ask questions on how to become a Christian.

You 'step out in faith' and begin your new life (Born Again see John 3:3-7).

Then the day arrives when you accept Jesus into your life and you are on the start line of your journey to Heaven as a Christian.

The course will test your Scripture study training, your physical endurance, and your dedication to continue to the end.

~~~~~~~~~~~~~~~~~

It has been said that the difference between a 'jogger and a runner' is the signed race registration form.

The difference between 'religion and Christianity' is your name written in the 'Book of Life'.

*"And anyone whose name was not found recorded in the **Book of Life** was thrown into the lake of fire."* (Rev. 20:15)

Runners are sometimes surprised at the difference between *'just training'* and going the distance under pressure. Once at the start line of a marathon, *'the distance of 26.2'* will soon become a shocking reality to many - and many, sadly enough, will not complete those miles.

Christians will often be surprised how hard it is *'to stay on course'* - *how many emotional injuries will be felt, the spiritual ups and downs of the course, and of the cost of being a Christian in this unsaved world. And, sadly enough some will fall away, they will give up and return defeated.*

Here are some great Scriptural truths, from various translations, that I enjoy reading and sharing.

"Don't you realize that your body is the temple of the Holy Spirit, who lives in you and was given to you by God? You do not belong to yourself." (1 Corinthians 6:19 NLT)

[One of the running clubs that I belong to is called **'4 His Temple'**. That verse is the club Scripture.]

"Do you see what this means – all these pioneers who blazed the way, all these veterans cheering us on? It means we'd better get on with it. Strip down, start running – and never quit! No extra spiritual fat, no parasitic sins. Keep your eyes on Jesus, who both began and finished this race we're in. Study how he did it. Because he never lost sight of where he was headed – that exhilarating finish in and with God — he could put up with anything along the way: Cross, shame, whatever. And now he's there, in the place

of honor, right alongside God. When you find your-selves flagging in your faith, go over that story again, item by item, that long litany of hostility he plowed through. That will shoot adrenaline." (Hebrews 12: 1-3 MSG)

"...run with perseverance the race marked out for us. Let us fix our eyes on Jesus, the author and perfecter of our faith..." (Hebrews 12:1-2)

"Press on toward the goal to win the prize which God has called me heavenward in Christ Jesus." (Philippians 3:14)

"Exercise daily in God - no spiritual flabbiness, please! Workouts in the gymnasium are useful, but a disciplined life in God is far more so, making you fit both today and forever. You can count on it. Take it to heart." (1 Timothy 4:7b8 MSG)

"You've all been to the stadium and seen the athletes race. Everyone runs; one wins. Run to win. All good athletes train hard. They do it for a gold medal that tarnishes and fades. You're after one that's gold eternally.

I don't know about you, but I'm running hard for the finish line. I'm giving it everything I've got. No sloppy living for me! I'm staying alert and in top condition. I'm not going to get caught napping, telling everyone else all about it and then missing out myself." (1 Corinthians 9:24-27 MSG)

"...athletes cannot win the prize unless they follow the rules." (2 Timothy 2:5 NLT)

A Two Dog Night

I'll tell you runners who are in my age bracket that - **no** – the title on this page is not a misprint as I am **not** writing about the rock group *3 Dog Night* that was popular between 1968 and 1975. And - **no** - it has nothing to do with the meaning of having 'a three dog night'. For those who do not know that meaning, here it is:

Having a 'three dog night' refers to being very cold. When cowboys out on the range had to share body heat, they referred to how cold the night was on a scale of 'a one-dog night' to the coldest being 'a three-dog night'.

The night that I am writing about is one that is far more exciting! It has nothing to do with singing and nothing to do with being cold. In fact, it happened on a very hot and humid night in central Florida while I was doing my nightly run.

While running down the street at about a nine minute pace, I was suddenly surprised by a medium sized dog darting past me. Other than being a bit startled, I just continued. Within a few minutes, a van pulled up along side and a woman yelled out the window *"Have you seen a dog run by here?"* I answered back that I just had and that I would try to help locate it. As the van pulled away, I went into jog mode and returned to the area that I had just covered running.

Getting into the spirit of the hunt, I started to weave in and out of driveways and up side streets and then noticed a dog up ahead on a lawn. I began to walk and called out to it. The dog came to me and I quickly recognized it to be a pug type dog - a lot smaller than the one that dashed by me before.

This dog was very friendly and was easily encouraged to be picked up. *"Now what do I do with this dog?"* I wondered. I felt that this kind of dog probably does not walk around by itself at night – in fact, we have a leash law. At this time, I noticed a young women walking toward me, so I asked her if she knew if this dog lived in this house. She said that she did not know and continued walking.

I checked the time and it was close to 10:30, maybe too late to knock on a door, but I felt it was worth the gamble to help this dog. An elderly man came to the door (I am 63 so when I say that someone is elderly, they are a lot older than I am!). Anyway, he said that his dog was watching "Gone with the Wind" with him. He looked over and said loudly *"He is gone! How did he get out?"* Taking a second look at me and at the dog in my arms, he recognized the dog was indeed his and said, *"Praise the Lord! Thank you!"* Soon I was back on the street in search of the 'runaway dog'.

As I headed back to the street, I heard barking. I looked ahead of me and there was a dog that looked like the one I'd seen earlier. I walked toward it and it turned and ran away – away toward the main street that had heavy traffic even at this time of night.

Another plan was needed. I stooped down low and called for it to come to me. It stopped running and slowly came toward me. When it got about 10-15 yards away, it stopped. Time seemed to stand still as we stared at each other. I prayed that the couple would drive by and help before the dog turned and got hit by a car.

Within 4-5 minutes, I heard the women calling to me from across the median dividing the street. She got out and called the dog – and as the dog ran toward her, a car came toward the dog. I ran into the street and waved the car to stop. She picked up the dog and called over to me again. I was thanked and asked my name. After telling her this information and answering a few questions about my running, I gave her one of my cards and told her to check out my blog: www.therrrick.com.

And so, this is my story that I jokingly share with others as the night that I may not have shared the Gospel, but two dogs were saved!

The Invitation

The invitation, at first, seemed a bit strange; maybe even a bit corny. It was the same as the title of that day's message, but seemed suddenly more personal. The invitation, printed on a rather plain 8 ¼ x 5 ½ off-white piece of paper had been neatly folded and placed within the weekly LifePoint church flyer. It was an idea that the pastor was trying out to draw attention to the message he was going to give. I listened closely to that message, even took notes – but why, I wondered, was it affecting *me* so much.

The wording opened another door in my life. I soon realized that the message had cleared the path to the door of my heart. My heart that I thought had been open – I realized had not been open completely to this Scriptural truth. On the outside flap, he'd written:

"You're Welcome…
…To Bring Your Pain"
The wording inside, however, just about took the
door off the hinges:
"We accept you…
… Just the way you are.
Jesus & Life Point
"Are you tired? Worn out? Burned out on
religion? Come to me. Get
away with me and you will recover your life."
(Matthew 11:28 MSG)

I thought about my running and writing ministry. I wondered if the Holy Spirit was guiding me to a better understanding of something in my life – if I was receiving a message to not only help me, but help others with whom I shared the 'Good News' across our country. Had I missed sharing something while I was witnessing to them?

As I reflected upon the notes that I had written while listening to Pastor White speak, the musicians began to play. **Then...**

My heart began to race within me! I was overcome by a flood of joy! I began to praise the Lord in song, prayed aloud in tongues and danced before Him! As the closing song was being sung, so much became clear to me about the urgency of *that invitation*! I wanted to proclaim **the invitation** and its special message to both saved and unsaved people as I witnessed and shared my testimony.

"Everything that goes into a life of pleasing God has been miraculously given to us by getting to know, personally and intimately, the One who invited us to God. The best invitation we ever received!" In addition, shortly after that, Scriptures tells us – *"So friends, confirm **God's invitation to you**, his choice of you. Don't put it off; do it now. Do this, and you'll have your life on firm footing, the streets paved and the way open into the eternal kingdom of our Master and Savior, Jesus Christ."* (Read 2 Peter 1:3 and 2 Peter 1:10 MSG for the complete verses / *bold* emphasis is mine). These *particular scriptures* flashed through my mind as clearly as if they had been written on the overhead screen.

We do not have to wait to heal, take care of our mistakes or solve our emotional problems. NO! Another part of the message was *"Brokenness does not disqualify me – It qualifies me!"* It is not like training for a race where you have to heal first and get your strength back – *before* you race. Failures, disappointments and discontentment can be thrown aside and replaced with clean cloths! Fresh running gear! This place, God's house, is the place to come with your pain, questions, broken dreams and relationship problems.

The words of praise surrounding me lifted me up even higher! They encouraged me to share this message – **this special invitation** – with as many who would listen outside the churches of America. I could not sit or just stand – *'gotta* *run'* were the words that I was clearly hearing! I was not even sure if they were the words from the song being sung or were flowing from within my spirit. I just heard them and wanted to share this message of joy. I felt freer than ever before to dance, sing, and to soon joyfully run with this power of praise and song upon my lips. I will be *crying out praises to Jesus – my Savior – my God, whose mercy reigns,* to as many people as I can.

That invitation I received, printed by someone at church, was surely originally authored by Jesus Himself. Moreover, it is as refreshingly new as the day He first offered it so many years ago.

The La-Z-Boy© Zone

Many people in America know this brand name. I also believe that most of them have the same mental, if not physical, pull when they see the name (or the recliner itself). The product image draws you into its peaceful zone – words are not necessary to convince you.

The word 'lazy' generally takes on a negative meaning; maybe that is why they spell it the way they do. The recliner name is not a negative one - it is just smart marketing with its implied invitation that you be 'La-Z' once in a while. And, to be able to own one – well, we find a way to pay the cost. **The cost may be more than you think if** you fall into that 'La-Z Boy© zone' too often.

As runners, we will pay these costs in ways not clearly seen as we first sit within its comfort. Its name will become clearer with each '*visit*'. While driving home from work, the '*La-Z-Boy zone*' will have its power over your thoughts. Excuses will form that will cause you to skip your daily run or workout at the health center. The list will be easy to form: had a hard day at work, am not feeling well, need to spend quality time with the family, a TV show I need (want) to view, had a bad night's sleep – need I go on? All or some of the reasons may be true. Nevertheless – they were true **before** you purchased that comfy chair and you **still went for your run or workout.**

After reading *inactive* as the definition for *lazy*, I felt led to do a word study. Let us take a quick look at some *synonyms* of the word *lazy*. I will list a few of the many words found on the web page of **Roget's New Millennium™** — *comatose, dallying, idle, lifeless, procrastinating, unenergetic and* *heavy-footed.* These words paint an unpleasant picture of a person in the recliner – words the manufacturer would not use in an ad!

Christian runners have another angle on that picture. Other words from Roget's thesaurus paint a picture of **another kind of cost.** The words **indifferent, neglectful, and apathetic paint a darker picture - especially the word - apathetic. Synonyms for that last word fall on too many Christians today.** How many of us are 'un-Christians'. We are **un**feeling, **un**interested, **un**moved and **un**concerned at times.

My pastor gave a great series of teaching about the recliner theory. You might want to obtain it (www.lifepoint. tv). He spoke symbolically of how so many of us are drawn to and enjoy the La-Z-Boy. Symbolically, we enjoy 'laying back'. We stay within the company of Christians – avoiding contact with those outside the fellowship of believers. The cost is time not spent being a *'light' in the community* - a witness to those *'outside our comfort zone'.* Scripture clearly teaches us about the 'Great Commission' (Matthew 28:16-20). Yes! We are to GO and share the *'Good News'.*

The Greek word for gospels is evangelion, which also means 'good news', since they retold the 'good news' of Jesus redeeming a fallen world. Each of the books reveals, through the story of Jesus Christ's life, the "Good News" about His presence in the world. The word gospel can also have a narrower meaning...the specific actions of Christ which are necessary for salvation.

The next time you look at a *'La-Z-*Boy' think of more than sitting on it or of the cost to purchase it. Prayerfully remember the cost of being in its comfort zone. If you already have a 'La-Z-Boy', invest your time on it toward praying for those with whom you will share the "Good News'. Runners remember this verse from Romans 10:15b: "How *beautiful are the feet of those who preach the good news."*

I will close with this wonderful translation of Romans 10:14-17 from The Message© by Eugene H. Peterson. May it bless and encourage you.

> *"But how can people call for help if they don't know who to trust? And how can they know who to trust if they haven't heard of the One who can be trusted? And how can they hear if nobody tells them? And how is anyone going to tell them, unless someone is sent to do it?*
>
> *That's why Scripture exclaims, a sight to take your breath away! Grand processions of people telling all the good things of God!*
>
> *But not everybody is ready for this, ready to see and hear and act. Isaiah asked what we all ask at one time or another: 'Does anyone care, God? Is anyone listening and believing a word of it?' The point is: Before you trust, you have to listen.*
>
> *But unless Christ's Word is preached, there's nothing to listen to."*

K.I.S.S.

Most of my articles end up being around 700 words long (maybe 'long' is not a good word choice here!). This works out well because of the newsletter space allotted to each article and for the BIGGER picture that was within my heart: this devotional book. I want to strengthen and encourage the struggling Christian runners, enlighten the 'religious' (as I was) who may err in thinking that they are on the correct course to Heaven, and to those runners who may not be giving any thought to their salvation.

Trying to be brief and at the same time complete in sharing what is upon my heart is difficult. People who know me know that I love to talk! Writing for me is just *talking on paper*. Writing allows me to feel close to people. I hope that it will bless my readers with a better knowledge of what runners go through in their training, races and life. In addition, I hope that the readers will better understand what Christianity is, compared to what people often think it is. Prayerfully, the readers will move forward with a better outlook on life, will have a closer walk with God, and will get greater enjoyment being part of the sport of running. I hope that many will *'step up'* their efforts to share their Christian faith too.

K.I.S.S. popularly means '<u>K</u>eep <u>I</u>t <u>S</u>imple <u>S</u>tupid'. I will replace 'Stupid' with 'Saints': <u>K</u>eep <u>I</u>t <u>S</u>imple <u>S</u>aints. A quick note – in the New Testament the word 'saint' refers to every Christian believer.

Whether it is in conversation or in an article for a running magazine, runners use terms that often confuse non-runners or new runners. Words we choose to explain something often 'leave others in the dark'. Words like *fartlek, electrolytes, gait*, or terms such as *speed intervals, oxygen debt, lactate threshold, PR*, and *explosive plyometric* are understood, in part, sometimes. Nevertheless, all too often people *'mentally run away'*. They say to themselves or to the person talking

"What in the world are you saying (writing about)? I just want to understand how to become a better runner!"

Christians often make this same mistake. They try to share why they are Christian, or what Christianity is, by offering very few or no understandable answers.

At my church (LifePoint), one of Pastor Brad White's sermons inspired this chapter. Some of his points clearly apply to both Christianity and running. In both cases, words written or spoken are often too long, *fussy* (full of details), *fuzzy* (full of fluff) and the *spirit of superiority* is **falsely** felt. A well meaning Christian can **cast a dark shadow on religion**. Terms such as *Jesus saves, the atonement, born again, washed in the blood* and *convicted* are understood by the speaker, but leave others **confused or 'turned off'**.

While web surfing for information for this article, I came across a few comments that can nicely close out this line of thought.

> *"God isn't looking for someone to change mankind's mind with words of wisdom and phrases that sound great but mean little, instead 'God hath chosen the foolish things of the world to confound the wise'! (Cor. 1:27) God doesn't want us to change their minds, He just wants us to be faithful and speak His Words and He will do the changing."*
> Clint Nobles / The Simple Message©

In Eugene H. Peterson's translation of the Bible, we read *"The message that points to Christ on the cross seems like sheer stillness to those hell bent on destruction, but for those on the way to salvation it makes perfect sense."* (1 Cor. 1:18a MSG)

Whether you are sharing how to run better or sharing the gospel – just use simple understandable words. As my pastor wisely said in that great message, *"Your words TODAY can impact someone's FOREVER."*

I personally recommend that you make it a conversational 'KISS' they will treasure and remember.

Expectations Beyond Your Limits

Your expectations, *what you thought you could do on your own,* **were beyond your limits; you felt captive – powerless** as *'an egg within a vise'*

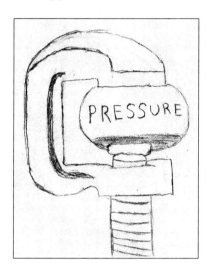

Drawing by Kourtney Parramore

The pressures of life had a clear hold on you. There seemed to be no space between *yesterday* and *tomorrow.* You were running and caught between the start line and the finish line. This situation, the one you put yourself into, had you praying with what symbolically seemed to be your last breath. **The unhealthy pressure of it all was about to test your limits.** You knew that God made us to strive and the key is selection. Your selection, the way you were living – *'running through life'*, was **not** going to be a success story. **No victory** was in sight.

As time goes on, you weaken, feeling the squeeze between the two points. Your lungs feel as if they will explode! More time goes by – you have no power to stop it; you only have control of how hard you press on. The feared marathon wall is there; you feel as if you can barely move. **The running manuals did not prepare you for this.** You didn't read about it because you thought you were smarter than others. Too late now to read and make other plans – you have been needlessly caught off guard. Your immediate thoughts are to find a way to release the pressure before you break down mentally and physically.

However as you continue to struggle in this situation you remember the *other book,* the one that did warn you about such pressures and the damage they could cause. You remember what you should have done BEFORE this day - BEFORE things got this bad on the course you had chosen.

These words often spoken in jest: *"When all else fails, read the manual"* do not seem funny now. The words in the Bible provided the answer. Those words seem to shout as loud as the crowd lining the street around you. That same crowd is watching to see if you will **'crack or fall'** and **be finished** right before their eyes. You clearly look pale – *as white as a ghost* – and about done for the day. Their cheers are a mixture of *"Hang in there!"* and *"Give up – you're finished!"*

The Scriptures instruct us to rest one day of the week (Ex. 34:21). Even the animals were given a day to rest! Do we think that we are better than God? He rested on the seventh day (Gen. 2:2). Matthew 11:28 comforts us with these questions and answers –

"Are you tired? Worn out? Burned out on religion? Come to me. Get away with me and you'll recover your life. I'll show you how to take a real rest. Walk with me and work with me – watch how I do it. Learn the unforced rhythms of grace. I won't lay anything heavy or ill fitting on you. Keep company with me and you'll learn to live freely and lightly." (MSG)

It becomes clear that you did things **your own way** - set **your own limits** - as you struggle to even hold up your own weight. You forgot that your body is the temple of the Holy Spirit (1 Cor. 6:9). You need to learn to protect the life within you.

You feel like Job and laugh as you recall the verse with the question *"Does anyone want the tasteless white of an egg?"* (Job 6:6b NLT) You feel like that *egg in the vise*. You **do not** want to crack under this pressure. You pray as you have not in a long time – you call upon the ONE, the ONE whose promise is still for today – *"Even there your hand will guide me, your right hand will hold me fast."* (Ps. 139:10 TNI)

The Christian message that I hope I conveyed here is that sometimes pride blinds us. I ignored the voice of experience in the runner's manuals and of my friends' experience in the running world. I also did not combine running rules with my faith nor did I see that the messages from each are complementary. The warnings were clear but I did not properly prepare. I let the pressure around me block out the truths. I held myself in that symbolic vise.

Although I performed poorly against my own expectations because of my failure to prepare, *I did find peace and renewed faith through the lesson learned. I was released from the power of that vise and I can see the way to the 'final finish line' a lot clearer now! I feel whole, strengthened and steadfast.*

Warning From a Senior Citizen

For runners of any age, certain cautioning rules should apply. However, they should emphatically apply to the *senior citizens who are* still 'up and running'. I will strongly add that without a doubt, *"God help them"*, the rules should be explained and reinforced to all the males and females at and over the age of sixty! Having recently reached the milestone age of 60, I recognize the value of reinforcing the rules for any runner who has also reached this point in life.

DO NOT drive long distances while on an antibiotic. This does not mean that you can skip your meds a few times in order to make the drive to a marathon that may be ten to twelve hours away.

DO skip the race if the temperatures are going to be extra hot! You can always do the race another year.

DO NOT push your luck during the winter months. When you see that all the *rooms* are filled, do not decide *"I'll try anyway and just see."* You have a good back up plan to have a blanket and pillow in the trunk, right? WRONG!

DO think twice and pray hard about doing practice runs (of any distance) during the summer months! Check out the temperatures for the day on TV or radio. You also might want to re-think your scheduled plans for the day and *not jog or race. If you run a race like Death Valley Borax Marathon, (that name should give you a big hint!) be ready to run in both below freezing temperatures and temperatures that will melt your socks!*

DO NOT even dream about filling forty-two months with thirty-eight marathons, three half-marathons and lots of shorter races. It will cause you nightmares just thinking of the money for gas, race applications and sneakers! Do not think that you are *'The Peter Pan Man'* who never gets old. Just because crossing finish lines will earn numerous trophies, ribbons and plaques – well, miles do add up and take their toll on the body.

LAST BUT NOT LEAST: DO NOT *pay attention to the advice I have written so far — I have proven it false. Well maybe you DO need to apply the rules if you want to avoid a lot of pain and stress.*

My running record proves that dreams do come true! I have proven that the Christian faith I have shared over the years has provided me, and many others with the inner strength and courage to go the seemingly endless extra miles that need to be run hard and fast. I have had great joy running - - thanks, in part, to being a member of a local running club and two marathon clubs. When I first moved to North Carolina and took up running again, the Salisbury **R**owan **R**unners (SRR) Club encouraged this 'then fifty-ish' guy with an invitation to membership, which included training and fellowship. The **SRR** was truly a blessing during those years — I miss those runners very much.

FOOT*note:* **DO** *listen to your body* when it tells you that you are healthy, happy, young, free and alive. Prayerfully go for a walk, jog or run when it calls out to you to do so! Keep it happy with healthy food and rest. OK – see a doctor for a physical to keep the family happy!

You will live healthier and fuller years than others say you can. You will have more miles behind you than they have **excuses** (OK **– reasons expressed in concern** because people cared) for not doing them! The sun will seem to come up sooner each day and your days will seem much shorter.

Enjoy adding to your scrapbooks and looking at your well-deserved awards! Let these things be an encouragement to others as well as to you – the one who had the courage to continue down the roads adding mile upon mile.

"GO!"

The voice inside you is sometimes *gentle* and others times *overpowering* like the roar of a lion. If that inner voice of yours is anything like the one that tries to get my attention, it is loud and very demanding! I'm sure you understand what I mean! You are minding your own business - maybe reading a magazine or viewing a TV show and **BAM**! A suggestion (or command to do something) is received. Maybe it does not have to be done right away, but you must make plans to do it. Hours, days or weeks later, you recall that idea and it pulls at you. You need to put the idea in *'the dead idea file'* or carry the idea through. *Been there - done that – have the t-shirt to prove it*! Another t-shirt — just what I needed!

Was it that inner voice that got you started in the sport of running? Perhaps a voice from within you (or from a close friend in conversation) moved you to take action. Result: today you are active as a runner! Maybe you do a few miles a week; maybe a lot of miles and compete. Either way – you are part of a healthy group who know how to enjoy life. Your days, maybe as a couch potato, have been blessed by the motivating word "**GO!**" Your days are more meaningful and life *'is an open road'* of adventure.

That decision to become a runner did, and still does, have a price tag. You needed to purchase the correct running gear. Your eating habits needed to change, your time had to be scheduled differently in order to train and maybe compete in races; and your circle of friends soon changed. Indeed, your lifestyle changed a lot. Today you can say with pride – *"I am a runner!"*

A number of people ask me why, at my age (63 now in 2008), I bother to strain my body and budget by traveling to all the states. They see my pain with osteoarthritis and they know of the many injuries that pull at my body. In addition, people wonder at the time needed to do all the marathons and think about the time I have to be away from my home. These good questions were (and are still) easily answered. I not only read, but also clearly heard the word **"Go!"** when I was reading scriptures. **'The Great Commission'** — Jesus' words still telling Christians today to **'Go'**. The most familiar reference is in the Gospel of Matthew (28:16-20). Those verses tell us to *'step out in faith'* and share the *'good news of the gospel'*. Words in the Book of Acts (1:8b) birthed my ministry. With this verse, I strongly felt led to run marathons in all of the fifty states sharing the 'Good News of the Gospel':

> *"...and you will be my witnesses in Jerusalem and in all Judea and Samaria, and to the ends of the earth."*

I put together a card to pass out which I often refer to as - *'God's business card.'* It looks like this:

Rrrick Karampatsos
jogandrun4fun@yahoo.com
Running Across America
Joyfully Sharing the "Good News'
"...run with perseverance the race marked out for us. Let us fix our eyes on Jesus..."
(Read Hebrews 12:1-2)
www.therrrick.com

My blog has some of my articles, information about my son Pastor Jason's church and about my church (LifePoint), and it has links to the web pages of some running clubs. The blog also has a 'Statement of Faith' and a section with PayPal, for those who feel led to support this ministry.
It is helpful for me to pass out this special card to runners and other people that I get a chance to talk to on the trips. I

ask them *to email any prayer request, ask for marathon race information,* and to *drop me an email note* from time to time to share what is happening in their lives. I am happy that many have done so.

I am constantly being blessed and able to bless many people, because - I **not only** listened to that voice, **but also obeyed,** both it and the Scriptures' call for me to - **"Go!"**

Voices Along the Way

This article's message laid heavy upon my heart for a number of days. The subject of *'voices being heard'* was birthed at a *'Life Group'* party during a conversation with a woman named Debbie. She was sharing with me about the time she ran her first 5K race and – well, I will do my best to share what she said.

*When I crossed the finish line of that 5K, I was angry. Angry because I had listened to others and told myself that I could not do such a thing as run a 5K race and finish it. I had finally tried and succeeded over the advice / comments given. I would **never – ever** again listen and accept, as fact, **negative voices.** I wondered often since then just how many things in my life I could have done **if I** had **only tried.***

The next few days I did research on 'hearing negative voices' at a Google® site I frequent. The www.crossway.com site highlights Christian quotes and articles. Of the many that I came across on this occasion, the following article (in part) sheds light on my subject from an interesting source.

The article by David Burchett is - **Are You Hearing Voices?** It provides a great example about 'negative voices' - voices that all too often come from our closest friends:

"My primary source of income is television sports directing…Reading the positive reports from spring training (Major League Baseball's Texas Rangers) has me excited about this season. I picked up the paper today and found a 'Peanuts' cartoon that hit the nail on the head on a couple of levels. Peanuts creator Charles Schultz loved the Lord and loved baseball….

This particular strip has Charlie Brown standing on the mound ready for the first game of the spring. Charlie Brown loves baseball more than any other character on the planet... Charlie raises his arms in triumphant joy and exclaims. 'I love the start of baseball season.'

In the next panel, he has a nostalgic smile and notes, 'There's a certain indescribable feeling in the air.' From the right field, Lucy decides to add her feelings about what is in the air: 'Defeat'.

Isn't that what most of us deal with from time to time...that voice from right field tells us that defeat is certain...."

It would be well worth your time to read the entire article.

I have personally heard such voices for many decades - decades filled with a seemingly endless number of accidents. I have shared about them in other chapters and will again later in 'The r-r-r-rest of the story' chapter. For now, I will just share this about the people around me during those accidents.

Doctors, relatives and friends often told me to *'not try so hard'*, *'accept the condition'* and the doctors declared more than once that I *'might not walk fully or at all again'*. Voices – voices that could have changed my life story - **but did not**.

Here is another example of voices from a different angle. Brenda Bates wrote the following devotional (www.InHisPath. com):

"For too many years I didn't even realize that I needed a Savior but in His loving and gentle way, He tapped me on the shoulder and whispered, 'Follow Me!' I listened to His voice, reread His love letter

(the Bible), and realized that He calls each one of us to follow Him. It is never the same time; it's in His perfect time. We are all given a special invitation to follow Him. Have you listened for His whisper? Have you felt the stirring in your heart that longs for more than what is here? Have you been awakened in the middle of the night and wondered why? Perhaps, just maybe, it's Jesus wooing you into a personal relationship with Him."

Jesus had to deal with the voice of Satan that tempted Him (Matthew 4) – a Bible study will show you numerous examples of people in the Old and New Testament that also heard the voice of Satan. We too will hear it. We are in a spiritual battle (Ephesians 6). There will be voices along the way to the final finish line – prayerfully test them.

Be as the sheep that Jesus spoke about in the Gospel of John (10:1-18) - *"...The sheep listen to His voice...they will never follow a stranger; in fact, they will run away from him because they do not recognize a stranger's voice."*

I am, and will be eternally grateful, that I did as Brenda Bates did - listened to, trusted and obeyed the voice of Jesus. He has since given me the strength to continue on the course that He has set before me. *"I can do all this through him who gives me strength."* (Philippians 4:13 TNIV)

Random Thoughts
(While running in pain)

Light rain mixed with temperatures in the mid 60s. A gentle breeze kept me refreshed, even with the rain jacket. Surprisingly, there was very little traffic during this hour of the morning. Overall, it should have been a pleasant setting for a long run. Should have been – could have been, if it was not for the pain in my left knee. That L2 sprain seemed to shout out for me to take a few more days off from running. Nevertheless, I had already taken a few days off and had done only easy jogging miles. The fact that the next marathon was only a few weeks away had me aware that I must get some miles in – pain or no pain.

Doctor Paton said I could run unless the pain got too bad. Hope the knee brace does not get too wet. What did he mean too much pain? Pain for one person may not be that much for another. I think that is one of the reasons that I do as well as I do running all these marathons - I am used to pain.

I will just jog and stay around a ten minute pace. Maybe the pain will not be as bad today as it – **OUCH,** *was yesterday.*

The Garmin® watch shows an 8:45 pace.

No wonder I'm hurting so bad! I better keep checking my pace or I'll be hurting so bad that I'll end up walking a number of miles back home again. **Ouch!** *Darn knee. The burning is bad enough, but the sharp pin like pain is almost too much to take – amazing that there is no pain when I walk. This is confusing — maybe a 9:30 pace.*

I think that I'll turn around at the Florida College parking lot. That's about six more miles. Knowing that Billy Graham went to school there is neat. There it is – time to get a drink at the fountain and then head back home.

If this pain lets up some, maybe I'll run over to the USF campus — that is always nice. Such a huge campus over - - ouch! – 9:05. Better slow down.

I really find it hard to believe that not even a year ago I was living in North Carolina, was running with the Salisbury Rowan Runners and was single. Now I'm living in the Tampa Florida area...and having USF and Busch Gardens just 2 -3 miles from where I live. Cool. So much has changed - ouch! I wish being in pain so often in my life would change. Wish this knee pain would change! Wish it would stop raining! Where is that Florida sun? Oh Lord! — This dampness and my arthritis – not a good mix for Rrrick.

The miles connect as each step is painfully recorded throughout the body. A Christian runner is pressing forward, faithfully training not only for himself, but as a testimony of *His grace and faithfulness* for others to see and to be encouraged.

Lord, thanks for listening to me rambling on and on while I ran today. Sorry for complaining about the pain – but, as You know, it gets quite bad at times. Even as I close out my run with this short prayer I am reminded how fortunate I am to be able to run at all – and, of those like Big Al, who are not able to run because of the extent of his injury. And, a great friend like Ed comes to my heart's mind at this time. I know that I would not be able to run as well without his helpful coaching. Even with him physically being hundreds of miles from here, I can still hear his encouraging words calling out to me.

Looking at my watch, I noticed that I have run 12.3 miles.

*OK – let's wrap up this run at a fast pace and get in 13 (**ouch**) miles. OK, a light walk to cool down probably makes more sense. Maybe the knee will not hurt as much* *tomorrow. Yes – maybe. Again I'll have to prayerfully rest on the thought that maybe tomorrow I'll be able to run without as much pain.*

As I walked to do a 'cool down', I thought back to my first race in April of 1999 and the pain that I'd felt in those last few yards heading towards that finish line. I remember the picture taken and the young guys around me seeming to wonder just "who is this old guy?" I placed 507th out of 2,246 that day. The pain was real – but the sensation of running in a race again was well worth the pain! Just like today – pain and at the same time, a wonderful feeling of *'life in motion'.*

Observer Marathon Festival
Charlotte, NC
10K 48:15
With photo courtesy of Marathonfoto.

Trapped Between the Lines

Picture yourself in this scene. You are feeling almost trapped as you race within a large group of fast-paced runners. They are within inches all around you and so close in front of you that what you see is their arms looking like pistons pumping away. Various singlet logos and messages are scattered before your limited vision and there is only an occasional chance to see their feet gliding before you. However, you still feel in control of the situation. Like an avalanche moving as one mass, you and your fellow runners quickly get beyond this early mass of bodies as mile after mile passes by.

Your legs are moving at a speed that is perfect for your targeted finishing time. Your heartbeat and pulse are under control and on target and hydration is no problem at this time. The start line is well behind you and the finish line as always will be there to cross once again. Nothing changes but the name of the race – even the pain is the same. However, as you move forward, that trapped feeling still holds you prisoner. As the runners spread out you are *free to run physically* – but are mentally '**trapped between the lines**'. Even with your love of running, you find yourself quoting from Thornton Wilder's great play, The Skin of our Teeth – *"Stop the world! I want to get off!"* Although it is clearly the same distance between the start and finish lines – you feel emotionally crushed and trapped between them. Yet, even as you are crossing the finish line, you will begin preparing for the next event and its racecourse cage. Just as you trained for your past races, you will again train and remain mentally and emotionally there, between the lines – trapped.

FINISH LINE

START LINE

Many of you have been in this scene. Perhaps the questions that came to your mind are similar to those that weighed heavily on mine; questions that tended to pull me down emotionally. The weight of unsolved issues– *emotional baggage* – was upon me. My heart could not function correctly because of the ever present pain. Spiritually I had a hard time to breathe in peace and joy. In fact, the joy of running was hardly with me anymore. As a Christian, I longed to cross over the final finish line into Heaven. Yes, I was tired of running *alone* in a crowd.

At the church service today, our pastor gave a great message about men feeling trapped. He shared about emotional pains not yet addressed or healed – and the fact that many of these problems stemmed from unresolved father-son issues from one's youth. My biological father left when I was three and my stepdad (who I loved very much) died when I was still a young man leaving me in a fatherless void. My problem **today** and maybe yours also, is the relationship with my Heavenly Father.

There were tears on my face from the song of praise we sang just prior to the pastor's message. The title –**You Rescue Me**© (Todd Anderson) – had set the stage as an answer for my pain. I knew that I had to go to my Heavenly Father to be rescued from my entrapment. Only then could I continue to *"run with perseverance the race marked out for us"* (Hebrews 12:1b) with joy again.

These three simple yet powerful words were taken home today: **acknowledge, allow,** and **ask**. These words spoke to me in a special way. The pastor's overall message was to accept the freedom that we can get only from God.

I had to **acknowledge** (and accept) my Heavenly Father's forgiveness, which I had continually sought for trying to run the race of life too much on my own strength and ability. I needed to **allow** His forgiveness to set me free from the bondage that entrapped me: worries about financing my ministry, worries about the people with whom I have shared the gospel and, heartache from the emotional wounds inflicted when my family members and Christian brothers and sisters question my running ministry. Yes! His forgiveness covered it all and I am able to freely move forward in His spirit and grace. I only had to **ask** my Heavenly Father to be with me and it was perfectly clear that by remaining in fellowship with Him I would never be alone.

How about you – the reader, runner, and redeemed of the Lord? Do you feel trapped between the lines in your life? If so, please apply the three words I have highlighted from the sermon by Pastor Brad White. We are all on the same course with the same salvation message to share. Accept your freedom, which was bought by the blood of Jesus – *"...and the truth will set you free."* (John 8:32)

Running *Naked* Across America

Pain within my body causes me to focus upon the areas that hurt while I run the miles during each marathon. I know the course of 26.2 miles will not be pleasant. I know that my logbook shows that I have run marathons in all of the 50 states, plus DC, but I still have many different marathons to complete in Florida. My ministry of *encouragement and the sharing of the' Good News'* has had extra needless stress placed upon it. The physical pain felt during the races as well as during the hundreds of miles of training and traveling seemed to be worth the cost. Our Lord entrusted me: spoke to me saying, "Go, share your testimony, encourage and be a witness of My grace and Love". I have done that, by His strength, in 50 states during this short time of 7 years of ministry. I am blessed with knowing that I am serving Jesus; that my Christian friends are with me in spirit and prayer each mile of each course when I am away from home.

Sadly, I have to confess my sin of doubt and fear. Another pain is slowing me down – one that is worse than what I feel with my arthritic hands, legs, feet and back. In fact, I am having a difficult time *'pressing forward'*. I am embarrassed when asked who is supporting me. I am too ashamed to tell them the truth. This emotional pain is far worse than the physical – I am embarrassed about being forced *to run naked*.

The missionary field that spreads from coast to coast is tough enough to physically cover alone. The hours driving to and from the marathons (drove 13 hour each way for the 2005 Arkansas Marathon – 26 hours to run 26.2 miles!) and the hours waiting in airports, in flight, driving to and from the race headquarters and motel rooms are many. The financial cost is a burden feeling like a backpack that is never taken off. All these facts are stripping me *down to the bare fact* that I feel as if I have only the covering of the prayers of my closest friends to go along with mine.

I am asked why I do not eat with my fellow runners, why I take flights so many hours before or after a race, or why I do not stay an extra night after a difficult race – such questions hurt and rob me of what joy I am holding on to and trying to share. In all of these situations, I do my best doing what I came to do in the first place. I pray for enough strength to be able to witness as an *ambassador for the Lord*. When, at the same time, I feel more like a beggar on the streets.

I know that my Lord knows and He sees what I am going through. I try not *to lean unto my own understanding* – but still, I fall short upon this course before me. Worse still – I sin failing in faith and move slowly forward in doubt. The prayers for my needs overshadow my prayers for others. In addition, when I return home, my heart wants to avoid any fellowship. To use a line from an old song – *I feel alone in the crowd*; no different from being away.

This is my confession and testimony of how I feel about this *ministry of encouragement and running*. It is being shamefully done - **symbolically naked** - *before God;* and in the presence of all the saved and unsaved I see each and every day of this ministry.

~~~~~~~~~~~~~~~~~~~~~~

I wrote this *after attending a service* where I saw a flyer on an upcoming message series: The Human Race – Go the Distance©. The second part of the series is titled The Human Race - **Run Naked**. Pastor Matthew Hartsfield (www.vandyke.org) gave the message series. *As seen above, I symbolically feel that I am.*

brightroom, Inc. 4/12/2007 Washington, DC

Night of the Navigator

It was dark and I was out for my long training run. Living in the Tampa, FL area for the past two years has made it difficult for me to train. Being a 'Boston area Yankee' the southern humidity is often 'just too much' to run in. A slow jog for three hours is about my limit. Often I am only able to get in 16 miles – and the miles are not very well done. However, the night miles are better than the 'junk miles' that are too often run during the hotter part of the day. I run and get the miles and time in but am never very sure of the value of the training.

Tonight, as I sit here getting my thoughts together for this article, I am still with emotion and stirred with many feelings about my time out on the local streets. Tonight I was blessed, humbled, and used – not three words typically associated with running; but all the same, three words that quickly come to my mind. My time and miles did not come close to what I had planned – but our Lord definitely guided those results. He knew what needed to be added to my training and the void that was in my steps. It was more than the hot temperatures, the lack of a breeze or the humidity. I was running in more than the dark of the night. The fact is I could not see where I was headed in my ministry. With each step, I felt the burden of my finances, the emotional pain of a troubled relationship, and the ever-growing doubt as to whether I was doing any good at all. With each step, I cried out *"Lord, help me see if I am on the correct course for serving You. Am I encouraging anyone anymore since I am not running marathons and can't even afford to run local races? Lord, am I wasting my time out here – is now just for my health?"*

I had stopped jogging and was walking at a slow pace. I was about to turn around and head back to our condo and just write it off as a bad night for training. I was not in the mood to even listen to the music – just not in the mood to be alone in the dark that was just too symbolic tonight.

Then it happened! A voice asked me how I was doing. A young man seemed to appear out of nowhere – I even thought for a brief moment that it was an angel! No, it was a young man walking from his car to one of the local homes. I was a bit embarrassed being seen walking – it is a runner thing!

"Tough night to run with the weather being like it is" I told him then added that I had a great run last Friday and... well – after a little sharing about running somehow I had mentioned marathons and sharing the 'Good News' in eighteen different states last year and all of the states and DC during the past six years. I have shared that so many times it almost 'just pours out of my mouth as a testimony'.

I soon found out that he is a student at the University of South Florida (two miles from my home in Temple Terrace) and was visiting his girlfriend. More important than that, he is a member of the Christian group called the Navigators*. Tonight he probably has no idea just how much he did for me in the way of clearly showing me the course that I need to continue. After our short talk, the exchange of e-mail addresses, and some insights – I felt clearer about the direction of my ministry and more assured that I was on course despite the 'troubled waters of life'. I was to continue to *encourage* other believers 'in the faith' as I had done these past six years – both on and off the roads.

With newly found energy, I began to jog. The stars seemed brighter and I even felt a breeze coming off the local lake! Although I did not jog many more miles, I felt complete in body and spirit. I wanted to get back home and make plans for what was ahead for me.

I am now satisfied with writing these articles, training, and being a witness on the local streets. I am at peace with my current problems – I clearly know that our Lord knows and cares. Gone is the worrying about what I cannot do in the way of marathons and other races thanks to the help of the *'navigator'* that the Lord put on my path.

*Check out: www.usfnavs.com

Worth It All!

There are a lot of costs associated with running a race whether it is a 5K, a marathon or for some of the fortunate ones able to do them, the ultras and triathlons. We runners add up these costs and ask ourselves "Is it worth it all?"

We have paid entry fees and the costs of traveling (flights, car rentals and the ever increasing gas costs) as well as the cost of the rooms. Even if we were lucky enough to share the cost of a room – well, it helped but there was still the meals to add to the overall cost.

I just had a flashback to a friend from Bartlett, Illinois – Don Pattison. He often brings his sleeping bag, sleeps on the floor between the two twin beds – yet, graciously pays a full one third of the room cost! Because of his great running ability, he still places very well in the races - even without a night's sleep in a bed!

Left to right:
Al Kohli, ME! and Don Pattison
(We were freezing – look at super man Don!)
Now where was I? Okay, back to my notes.

I would not be thorough if I omit the high cost of the running gear. For those who also have run a lot of marathons – maybe even one in every state and DC - the miles add up quickly and sneaker replacements are frequent. Some of the runners in the marathon clubs recall the lower cost of flights and entry fees; costs that have increased very much since the early days of the campaign that was launched to run in all 50 states and DC. Many have said that if they knew the cost would be so much they would not have set the goal to do all of the states. I have said it also – none of us really believes our own words! Once you start, it gets deep into you. The fellowship of marathon runners and the rush of doing the different state marathons make it well worth the overall expense. Yes, I know that for me it was definitely worth it all.

I have been blessed in another way too. I may be the only one who has achieved the goal of running in all of the states and DC - AND to share the *'Good News'* in all of those states and DC. To be able to do this has cost me more than time and money – more than just seemingly endless hours of training that we all have to do. To be able to even get to the very first starting line I had to rededicate myself to my Lord and Savior, Jesus Christ. In addition, I had to be healed more than once in order to walk and then run.

This is a scripture that has comforted me for years and now means more than ever before:

".. all things work for the good
of those who love him,
who have been called according to his purpose."
(Romans 8:28)

I mention that it means more now because now I can see my Father God's purpose of allowing all of the many accidents, operations, physical therapy, chiropractic visits and years of pain. If it was not for answered prayers and Jesus healing me, I would not have my testimony of encouragement to share with others as I witness to the blessing of being a Christian.

My witness is strong for I have a personal story to share, which took decades to unfold. Just like the poem 'Footprints' even when my faith was small and I sometimes felt alone in my pain Jesus was with me on this life course. His sacrificial pain on the cross convinced me I am able to continue to the final finish line.

Every accident, all the pain, every dollar and moment training and racing has been worth it all. Every marathon completed and article written and read by you was born before I even felt led to do this ministry. I have been able to turn over the soil, plant seeds and water (1 Cor. 3: 6-9) – and in faith I know that many souls have been harvested. I have been blessed to meet other Christians at races who went on to win souls, at least in part because of my encouragement that they too share the 'Good News'.

Praise the Lord! It was, and will be, worth it all!

"The r-r-r-rest of the story"

There is a certain voice that most people recognize when they hear it on the radio. The folks who know that voice also know that he will be saying – *"You know what the news is. In a minute, you're going to hear (*long pause*)...the r-r-r-rest of the story!" The voice* leads the listener down a road and as soon as you think you know where it is heading, the pause in this famous style invites you to wait – and you DO wait and anticipate what is to come. You almost feel compelled to wait. You want to know the 'rest of the story'. In time, we do know the ending of his story of a famous person, place or object. Paul Harvey is one of a kind as far as story telling goes. People have been blessed with his stories for many years.

I have used a number of his stories in my Sunday school classes, as well as a few that I put together, to draw the attention of the class so I could then focus the students on Biblical truths. The students came to know about *'the Good News'* in the Bible. Many of the junior high students were saved because they had not only heard, but also accepted the truth of the gospels. They were 'born again believers' wanting to hear (study) *the rest of the story.* They studied the Old Testament, which then pointed them to the New Testament and Jesus. Their faith, strengthened by knowing more facts, made them better prepared for the obstacles on the course of life.

My accent makes it easy for others to guess that I am a Yankee from the Boston area. Words with 'r' in them often cause folks to chuckle or ask, *"What did you say?"* As you may have noticed, the letter 'r' is in my first name three times! That was the result of a joke played on me by a sweet woman in China Grove, NC. It is one, of many events, that make up *the r-r-r-rest of my story!*

~~~~~~~~~~~~~~~

We each have a story to tell. Whether you are a Christian, or are satisfied with your own personal religious beliefs, **you have a story.** The main and *most important difference* will be **the ending of your life story.**

As I traveled from state to state in my quest to run a marathon and witness in each state, I shared how I began to run marathons. **My story,** which I have shared in bits and pieces in the earlier chapters of this book, is one with 'exciting' events like numerous accidents, operations, illnesses, and doctor's reports stating that I may never walk again. I share about the many bones that I have broken, being unconscious for 11 ½ days, the seemingly endless times in physical therapy, at chiropractors, and the times that I was in wheelchairs, on crutches, in body braces, or used a cane. I also share about the different medications that I used to be on and one that I still take for my crippling headaches.

The journal of my life includes stories of my *'push the envelope' sports adventures.* Times such as when I fell off a cliff while skiing and was caught in a net, or when I got caught in the coral reefs while snorkeling in the bay outside Puerta Viarta, Mexico because a rush of water within a cave I was exploring pulled me into the rough coral – numerous cuts and a bloody trail marked my retreat back to the ship. There is the story of when I was repelling on a trip, how I miscalculated and found myself helpless upon a narrow ledge, and yet another time while I was skin diving for lobsters up in New England and my air hose ripped!

Some of my running misadventures make me laugh as I recall them. A few examples of the funny ones are: the time I was chased by the coach of my cross-country team in a golf cart and pulled out of the race. Another was when I ran a race with the 14" pin – I placed 5th overall! BUT, it was in the sports section of the local paper and hurt my court

169

case! I was wild and lived for the thrill of running; I thought of no one but myself. It is true that I have done more things than the average person might ever dream about - but - the scary part of the stories is the fact that I was living out these adventures **within the shadow of the cross**. I was not saved back then. Hell was at all times only a breath away. My faith in a religion was not going to save me no matter how much I believed in it. Beliefs are not truths unless they are Biblically sound. *"A half truth is a whole lie."* It took years to find the 'truth'. I found it in the life of Jesus as I came to know 'why' He died for me.

There was a thread of Christian faith in the family I formed as an adult. That thread weaved us together into a patchwork story. The patches told of broken hearts, depression, financial problems, and questionable views about Christianity. To the outside world, we looked strong and firm in our faith. Underneath, yes, underneath, we were very much just pieced together; each was holding onto the best that each day would allow. We were all part of the same story, but each family member was affected differently. I personally found it impossible to remain firm in the faith because I was on my back so often. My family, at best, could only lean on each other. Jesus did not seem to be real; well, not like we had read and heard about. Church members offered words of comfort and encouragement, which, like our faith, seemed empty and sometimes just not enough to help us bear the pressure of our pain and heavily burdened spirits and bodies.

We each survived those years, but only because we came to truly know the love of Jesus. His grace enriched our Christian faith and that was enough to enable us to stay in the race toward that heavenly finish line. Each of our stories has many more chapters to be written before Jesus returns, or our heavenly Father takes us home. My four sons were repeatedly tested during their young lives and as young men now know just what it cost us as a family to reach the point where we now see our way to Heaven. I cannot run their race to the finish for them, but can pray and cheer them on!

Despite the lack of accidents and serious injuries in the past few years, I still have had to deal with a lot of pain. The physical pain has been because of damaged vertebrates in my spine, osteoarthritis in my body, and three 'in office procedures' to clear up the basal cell carcinoma, in my right ear. (*I had never thought of sunscreen on my ears! Do now!*)

One day while I was praying and writing about the excess of pain I experience, Scripture came to mind and it helped me feel better and more at peace. The answer was short and to the point. '**Lean not. Press forward**'. I knew that I should - "*Trust in the Lord with all of (my) your heart and lean not on your own understanding.*" (Prov. 3:5) - and that I needed to "*Press on toward the goal to win the prize for which God has called me heavenward in Christ Jesus.*" (Phil. 3:14). I was also reminded of the price that Paul paid in his ministry. Among other things, he was often beaten, shipwrecked, hungry, and cold. (2 Cor. 11:23-27). When I come across a tough hill during a marathon, I picture Jesus going up His hill to the cross. I think of the pain He willingly endured during those steps to the cross and know that He had the power to end the ordeal but did not do so. How can Christian followers complain with those images in their mind? How can they quit?

The sacrifice of Jesus made eternal life with Him available to us. Accepting Him as Lord and Savior places our name in that book of eternal life (Phil. 4:3; Rev. 21:27). It is up to us to take that very important step. No one else can do it for us. It is so simple a truth that many mentally trip over it. The result, as many of us know, is a needless hellish answer.

You each have a story. *What will the ending be?* Will Jesus know you and receive you at the end of your course in life? That question is more important than any story about my crazy past life. At 63, I continue to live a life which is full and exciting; and I do it with a youthful Christian spirit. My running adventures may be interesting. **HOWEVER, they are not as important as what you are NOW doing with YOUR life.** The answers to *"Where are you in your spiritual walk? Are you on the Biblically correct course? And, where will you spend eternity beyond that finish line?"* will define the **stories ahead of us.** I pray that something I have shared with you will strengthen and encourage you to press forward to get back on the track if you're strayed and will move more of you to join me in this great and victorious Christian life! In a race, all are called runners (whether we can move fast or, as The Penguin© - Jim Bingham says – "Start slow then taper off!"). My prayer is that everyone who hears me speaks or reads my book will be recognized by Jesus as a *Born Again runner.* I pray that the Holy Spirit will be allowed to use each and every one of us on this Heaven bound course; and, that we will all be moved to invite and draw many others along with us.

As interesting as they may be, the stories about my ministry of encouragement and sharing the 'Good News' across America fall faint in comparison to the main event in our spiritual life with its spiritual warfare. All of us are still writing **the r-r-r-est of the story** – we can, for the most part, control how it ends.

One is the Loneliest Number

When I was doing mostly 5Ks, I was a bit frustrated that I could not break 20 minutes. I was finishing with a 20:05, 20:03, then another 20:04 and even hit 20:00. But no matter how hard I tried, or what different ways I trained and ran the race, I still could not break 20 minutes. Yes, I placed well within the total numbers of runners; placed 1st most of the time in my age group which was 55-60 at that time. Nevertheless – **that one second** was out of my range of success UNTIL one race in which it finally happened! I ran a **19:59**. I was then ready to move on to the challenge of marathons, and soon marathons in all of the states would become a big part of my life as a runner. That **one second** *was a big number for me* – it redeemed me from what I felt was a failure in running 5Ks.

The same type of story is part of my marathon race times – I needed to break 3:45 to run Boston – I did not do it the first year. In fact, I just missed it by a few minutes! HOWEVER, I paid the price for that big push with a year and a half of physical therapy. Finally, breaking the needed time was happening regularly and in 2005, Boston was part of my marathon history. I will add here that in 2006 I even ran a 3:34 in Houston! I will remember that ONE!

Runners, especially long distance runners, like to race and train alone. I do, however, keep the Lord at my side. I have often wondered how many people are out there for that many miles and hours that are not in fellowship with our Lord – not in prayer for the **ones** in his or her life.

A friend told me that my marathon runs are a street ministry – a street ministry of 26.2 miles. It is true in a few ways, I guess. I am able to run and talk – many runners cannot. I am able to keep a pace that challenges many runners and encourages them to run a better race. My club singlets open many doors to conversation with questions that then allow me to give my testimony. I share about my healings, my Christian faith, answered prayers, and some stories about other runners and how they moved forward in their faith, with a better understanding of what is available to Christians.

I also witness going to the marathons with my 50 States Marathon Club, or with my 50 States and DC Marathon Group shirt or sweatshirt. They are great apparel tools to draw people into a conversation. I witness at the airports, on the plane, at the expos, and before and after the races in the finisher's area.

Many of you are familiar with the scripture story when Jesus spoke to the two criminals beside Him - in the last moments while dying on the cross. It made all the difference to both of them – one spent eternity in Heaven and the other in hell.

You may only witness to one or you may witness to many hundreds of people. What you say may make that difference of eternity versus damnation for one or many of them.

Because Jesus died on that cross for you and me, I believe it is my privilege (and obligation) to share the Good New of salvation with others. I hope you will share this belief.

Because one man cared enough for his salvation, D. L. Moody was saved. Think of the many people who were then saved through his ministry – some by hearing the message directly from him and others because those who heard him went on to share the truth with others. In each case, it only took one person to witness and one to receive.

I shared with some people about a period in my early Christian life that I had a healing ministry. I was often asked – "How many healed?" My answer: *"Two to my knowledge"*. I added that I was able to *'stand in'* for Jesus Who used my hands. I tried to make it clearly understood that the power was from Jesus.

"You call that a healing ministry! That is not many at all – what good is it if only two were healed? – I responded that

"*It was more than enough for the two.*" One of them could not breathe well and now sings for the Lord. The other has been free from back pain and can testify what God still does! It was one person at a time. Were there others? I will not know until I cross *the final finish line!*

I feel that I was, and still am, a part of more important healings – *spiritual healings*. We all can be part of that ministry. The greatest healing is the one which rids the body of eternal death – the one that frees the body of damnation - allows the body to be born again!

Here are a few other examples from scripture that focus on the importance of the number one. I list the parable story and its scripture and allow you to look it up later for a good Bible reading study time.

The Parable of the Lost Sheep (Luke 15 4-7)
The Parable of the Lost Coin (Luke 15:9-10)
The Parable of the Lost Son (Luke 15:11-31)
Ten Healed of Leprosy (Luke 15:11-19)

Bringing this subject up to more recent times, I will share that I only know of *one person* with whom I shared the *Good News* who was *Born Again* as a result of my effort.

Shortly after I was saved, one of my co-workers saw the difference in me. She had been searching also – but had started going to a local Kingdom Hall (Jehovah Witness). A tract about the Holy Spirit that I had passed on to her was the tool to break the chain of confusion.

It made all of the difference to her, her family and perhaps many others over the years. Her unsaved husband was dying in a local hospital. She witnessed and continued to pray for him. The night before he passed away he came out of the coma, accepted Jesus as his Savior, and another *'one'* entered into eternity with Jesus.

I will share the secret with you of how to be victorious in your witnessing: Be **prayed up** and just **show up. God will do the rest.** OK – you will need to know some key scriptures from time to time. HOWEVER, most often I only get to share my testimony – they cannot dispute that. They see living proof – my joy and excitement about Jesus is real to them. Some, when I have time, will listen to some scriptures. Although they will forget some of the testimony and the scripture, they will have heard the truth – seeds were planted, or maybe watered. I run to witness to as many as I am able. That is the number that is important - not my race time or the trophies.

Yes, I have won hundreds of trophies, plaques and ribbons – but, I am looking forward to *the final finish line* to see how many people are waiting for me and will join me in the winners circle with our Lord Jesus Christ placing the crowns upon our heads!

One is a lonely number. I do not want to - and will not - cross the final finish line alone.

Talking Along the Course

You might not remember my name, although the name **Rrrick** does seem to be remembered by many folks, but I am sure that you would remember me from a race. Not because I was fast, had fancy running sneakers or anything like that. No, it could be because I shared my testimony of how I was once paralyzed from the waist down; or how Jesus healed me the night before the operation that was to place a metal plate in my back. I would have shared how my faith has been since tested and about the spiritual warfare Christians are involved in every day. I may have passed a card to you that I call *'God's business card'* that has my blog and e-mail information as well as my name and address. I may have even asked you to e-mail me any prayer request that you had or a friend or family member may have. All of this would have happened within just a mile as I moved on, or dropped back, to witness to yet another runner during my *'marathon street ministry'*. You would have been one of the thousands that I was blessed to meet across the country, as I did all of the states and DC. The **name** that I wanted you to hear clearly and to keep with you as a source of comfort during the race was not my name, but the powerful **name of Jesus.**

Talking while running is not for every runner. I have had runners admit that they could not do both, others ask how I could talk so much and still run fast, and some have even asked me not to talk to them. Each wish was respected and the runner was prayed for either aloud or silently as I backed off in conversation and moved toward another runner.

There were always two good reasons to be at a marathon: to get the state checked off and to use all opportunities to witness and encourage runners. At many of the marathons, I was blessed to accomplish both.

At some of the races, I felt led to stop and ask runners who were obviously in pain if I could pray for them – most were open for the prayer. At many of the marathons, I have slowed down and even walked with runners who looked like they might not be able to finish. This usually resulted in a newly formed friendship that continues even today with e-mails containing updates on family, spiritual and race information. The time invested talking as we continued along the remaining miles was more important than any recorded race times. The same medal was given at the finish line.

Yes, I will have to admit that some runners were not kind with their comments about me talking – especially my talking about Jesus. However, I joyfully add that there were not many of them. I may never know if my prayer for them helped. I probably will not ever know if I was able to plant a seed or maybe just turn the soil of his or her soul for someone else to plant the seed. The fact remains that I tried and was faithful to my Lord.

During a marathon in Coeur d'Alene, ID I felt led to remain with a young man (maybe in his thirties) from Germany. We ran a steady nine minute pace for hours. During that time, he made it clear to me that he respected my view but believed that all religions lead to Heaven and that Christianity was no different from any other. I prayed silently for help from Jesus. That help came even as I was lifting up my need for some kind of wisdom or help.

A young teenage girl passing by us turned around and yelled out *"Jesus – I heard you say Jesus! I just got born again – I am saved – I am now a Christian!"* I excused myself, ran, and caught up to her. We prayed and exchanged a few words. When I slowed down and looked over to my German friend, I noticed a different expression on his face. I quickly said, *"That is the difference".* For the next few miles, we did not speak again about it. When we did talk, it was just a few words about our pace and the hills. I felt it was time to slow down and be used by God with another person. The pace and the excitement had drained me in a wonderful way. I had no doubt that both he and that girl would remember that marathon for more than one reason – one of them being the words I spoke to them about Jesus. I was able to fan the spiritual flames of that newly 'Born Again' girl - and, show the young man what a spark of the Holy Spirit will do to a person.

Who is at the center of your conversations? I am not being judgmental – just would like you to be blessed with the opportunity that Christians have during those miles and hours. **You** *can make a difference* to lighten the load of a Christian – or direct a person to the Final Finish Line in Heaven!

Photo taken by Steven Yee - Marathon Maniac #1

The Toughest Course

I have run a number of challenging courses in the seven years since I started running again at the age of fifty-six. The training and actual race miles have totaled over 14,000 miles.

Some of these races bring to mind the group *Blood, Sweat and Tears*. There was pain, and from time to time physical therapy along with a few visits to the Pain Clinic for spinal injections. I can clearly remember the days following those extra hard races when I kept asking the often hard to answer question *"WHY?"* Others have often asked us that also – right? For me the answer was clear. The moments of challenge at each and every step allowed me to feel very much alive, young and blessed by my Lord. A trophy was not sufficient to show what went into achieving the win. It could only show that my finish time was faster than someone else's. Although I was happy to win those trophies and to see them on a shelf at my home, in time each was moved to a box in the corner of my study. This is not so with my memories that remain with me as I train and race. I use the memories to remind me of my past mistakes such as *starting out too fast, not knowing the course better,* or even the fact that I all too often *played it safe* and only ran with the flow of the pack.

The **toughest course was not** the one that started with temperatures in the high 90s on back roads and through woods at night with only a flashlight to guide the way (Moonlight Bogie Marathon / Ellerbe, NC); nor was it the one in which snow and hail ruled the day – it was in the mid 80s when I left to drive up to the mountains with my summer running gear (Virginia Creeper Marathon / Abington, VA). I could, but will not say that it was the run up Grandfather Mt. in North Carolina (The Bear 5 miler) nor the ten miler that went straight up for the first half and then dropped down (*Woolly Worm Woad Wace / Banner Elk, NC*).

For many of you the words 'toughest course' might bring to mind the following races in the 5, 8 and 10K or half marathon distances we have run together! Great race names such as: *Ain't Hogs Great, Winter Flight, China Grove Challenge, Coon Dog Day, Bare Bone and the Gold Rush (Yes – we ran in a real gold mining area of Concord, NC!).* Each of these admittedly, had their particular challenges.

My marathon friends and I have struggled in some marathons right from the very first step to the *"Finally!"* finish line. The 2003 Jacksonville Bank Marathon comes to mind with its drenching rain every step of the way (I could have sworn I saw a few fish pass me while I was going up one of the hills!). In addition, I think of the marathon in the thin air of the mountain plains of Green River, WY where Phillip Griffith and I struggled 'step by step' with pain in our lungs. Then there were the extreme temperatures (from freezing to a blazing sun) during the marathon in Death Valley where Rick Bryson and I realized just what people went through years ago in that Borax 20 Mule Team© area. I could go on with a number of other marathons with their less than *ideal* conditions – but many of you know where the races were, and someone who ran in them.

HOWEVER, the answer to which was the toughest is not any of the above.

The **toughest course** was the one that **I did not fully respect. Can you admit that also?** Whether it is a 5K race or any distance up to a marathon, *the facts are the same.* We clearly know that **each course is different** – we also need to remember that each contains the same basic rules for running it – *preparation and respect.*

Every runner needs to prepare and apply the following for every practice run and race. *Prepare physically* with a proper warm up of a walk, easy jog or maybe even some gentle stretching. *Mentally* focus on form. Always cover your time with prayer and do not forget to pray for others in your life. Not just a quick one before you start – but, throughout the time that you are being blessed with the strength to run.

If you don't do these things, you may find yourself on that toughest course with damage to your body. Never take any step, any day, or any race for granted. Treat each with the caution that will allow you to finish the run safely.

Running Across America

America looks a lot smaller on the map now. Not too many years ago, six years to be exact, I had only been in thirteen states – all of which lined up on the East Coast. As I look at the map before me, I notice that I could fit most all of the states that I had visited into two or three of the larger ones out west! Because of the marathons that I have run in all of the states (and DC), I think of the *America* differently – I also feel an emotion deep within my heart as I read or say, *The United States of America.* The states, for me, are truly that - more *'united'* than ever. Running marathons on the many streets in the cities of each state has caused me to envision that we are like one large neighborhood. The runners and non-runners alike that I was blessed to meet have surely become an extension of the friends who live near me. I never could have learned this from reading or seeing a movie. *Step by step,* I became richly blessed and grew increasingly prouder to be a citizen of this great country.

With photo courtesy of Marathonfoto.
Finish Line at the Maui, HI Marathon

I am an American marathoner living with the freedom to run and share my Christian faith anywhere I wish. In my mind, I have symbolic footprints from marathons all over this country and I have only to imagine myself at any one of them to recapture the experience. The trophies and t-shirts, which I proudly wear, add to the overall experience. I gladly share information about the marathon, the city, the state and the people who live and work in the area. Although *'running across America'* in my *'senior years'* was more than I could have ever dared dream, it is now a reality. As I move forward with new adventurous marathons closer to home, I want to learn all about the people, cities and the state that I now call my home. *"Florida, get your cities ready for me to come and run your many marathons!"*

A question, I am often asked is *"What was your favorite marathon?"* When I had run only a dozen or so marathons, it was easy to have *'a few favorites'*: all the ones that were not run in snow or rain!

Now that I have run 57 marathons, I have a whole lot more marathons that were run in dry weather from which to choose favorites. Now **the problem** is this. How can I compare courses run in the majestic mountains to those within view of the Grand Canyon or one in Death Valley versus one that showcased the glaciers in Juneau, AK? How about the one on the High Plains in Wyoming versus the one on the paradise island of Maui, HI? Want more? Okay, what about the beauty of courses along the Atlantic Ocean versus the Pacific Ocean? Then there are the courses that were within so many of the beautiful cities of our great country – sometimes with tulips along the side of the street or mountains capped with snow that I thought I could just reach out and touch.

Okay, with so many marathons to evaluate as favorites, I probably want to delete the tough courses with hills that hurt as much going up as going down. There were marathons run in the 90s and some below freezing. Sometimes we were lucky to see anyone at all except at the start and finish lines. **But, my favorite?** Still too close to call.

I pray that **YOU** will dig deep within yourself and take the challenge to do as I did. Add your name to the '300 plus runners' who have completed this '50 States plus DC' challenge – some more than once! **Feel too old?** *I started to run marathons when I was 56!*

"What's in your wallet of confidence?" With the proper training, blended in with faith and prayer – ok, maybe a little luck also - you can claim your trophy for completing a marathon in all of the states! Check out www.MarathonGuide. com and the Running Journal www.running.net to find a few races that look interesting - and then sign up! See America *'one step and one marathon at a time'!*

With photo courtesy of Marathonfoto.
My 50th state, September 2007

Tired

I'm tired, Lord -
I'm tired of it all.
I'm tired of the high race fees.
I'm tired of spending all that money to get to the
marathons.
I'm tired of the high cost of the rooms.
I'm tired of the pain while training –
the pain during and after the race is over.
I'm tired of being depressed thinking about it all.

Father God -
I'm tired of trying to share my faith with the runners
who could care less.
I'm tired of hitting the wall at the start line of each
new day.
I'm so tired of feeling this way.
How can I be encouraging when I need to be -
what kind of ministry is this?
I am in debt financially and emotionally.
So few of the many thousands witnessed to and
encouraged respond;
none have I seen accept You as Lord.

Jesus –
The cost is too much to bear.
My wife is no longer -
at either line nor along the way as a spectator.
I am so tired of crying-
doing Your will alone.
My feet no longer want to run;
my lips are hesitant to witness and encourage.

Please, I pray -
assure me that this, Your Word, is for me:
*"...those who hope in the Lord will renew their
strength.
They will soar on wings like eagles;
they will run and not grow weary,
they will walk and not faint."*
(Isaiah 40:31)

Holy Spirit, sustain me to be able to...
*"...hold out the word of life – in order that I may
boast on the day of Christ
that I did not run or labor for nothing."*
(Phil. 2:16)

*"Are you tired? Worn out? Burned out on religion?
Come to me. Get away with me and you'll recover your life.
I'll show you how to take a real rest. Walk with me and work
with me—watch how I do it. Learn the unforced rhythms of
grace. I won't lay anything heavy or ill-fitting on you. Keep
company with me and you'll learn to live freely and lightly."*
(Matthew 11:28-30 The Message©)

Have <u>YOU</u> ever felt tired?
Do <u>YOU</u> now?
Please join with me in prayer as we rest in Him.

Father, I lift up my friend.
Allow that perfect peace that I have needed and
received so often,
to fall upon and comfort as only You can do.
Please help us to be renewed by Your Holy Spirit
as we press into You, and forward toward
the final finish line.
Guide us, I pray, with wisdom to draw
others with us.
Amen.

Directions

Often when I am running or driving up a steep hill, I remember a statement that a teenage boy said to me when I asked him where his house was: *"I live at the top of the hill – halfway down."*

Directions – they can be *simple to follow* or leave you **unsure** of what to do. This definition is one that I will use to further explain just where I am taking you in this article:

> "The line along which anything lies, faces, moves, etc., with reference to the point or region toward which it is directed: *The storm moved in a northerly direction."*
>
> Dictionary.com Unabridged (v 1.1)
> based on the Random House Unabridged Dictionary ©

I needed to know where to stop the car to drop Barry off at his house. The question was answered in such a way that I still remember the answer after over thirty years! However, at the time it was not of much help – I still did not know exactly where his house was.

Any of us, especially during the shorter races, has had to guess which way to go as we approached an intersection of two or more streets. I remember a race in which I was running way ahead of most of the runners and the only person in sight was a young man who was standing at the fork in the road. I waved and yelled out "Which way? Which way?" He just continued to stand still staring at me right up to the moment that I was only a few feet from him. I had to slow down and repeat the same question. Only then did he point the way to go. Directions, though given correctly, are not always given when immediately needed.

How many of us have been concerned during a marathon that we would not understand the way to go when the half marathoners were separated from the full marathoners? Worse yet, what about the runners doing the half finding themselves on the full marathon course? The bottom line is that too many of us have had to guess which way to go at many an intersection.

Spiritually speaking, the question of how to get to Heaven has unnecessarily been answered in confusing terms. It has also been given in misleading, non-biblical terms. The Bible clearly has the answer. God did not inspire men to write in such a way to confuse people with such important information. Satan is the author of confusion – we need to remember that.

Men (and maybe women sometimes) pour out energy to do something without reading the directions first. We often find ourselves backtracking and finally do read the directions. The saying, *"When all else fails, read the directions"* is ever so appropriate! Our directions for God's plan for humanity are written in the pages of the Bible. For people who try to do it on their own, it may become too late to read the divine directions. There will be no time for – *"When all else fails..."*

I like the tract Roman Road which clearly shows (directions) how to get to Heaven. It will help you with your personal journey, and by sharing its truths, will help others join you as you head 'Toward the Final Finish Line'

– Heaven. Here is a copy of what you can also find at: www. allaboutgod.com, reprinted here with permission.

Roman Road: The Highway to a Relationship with God

Roman Road – it's not just a systematic way to build highways inherited from the Roman Empire in the 1st Century. It's also God's plan of salvation set forth in Paul's letter to the Romans. Also known as, the Roman Road, the following is a collection of passages that build a beautiful and systematic approach to the gospel of grace by and through Jesus Christ.

Roman Road: The Gospel of Grace
Follow Me:

Romans 1:20-21: *"For since the creation of the world His invisible attributes are clearly seen, being understood by the things that are made, even His eternal power and Godhead, so that they are without excuse, because, although they knew God, they did not glorify Him as God, nor were thankful, but became futile in their thoughts, and their foolish hearts were darkened."* We must acknowledge God as the Creator of everything and accept our humble position in God's creation.

Romans 3:23 *"For all have sinned, and fall short of the glory of God."* We must all realize that we are sinners and that we need forgiveness. We are not worthy of God's grace.

Romans 5:8 *"But God demonstrates His love toward us, in that, while we were still sinners, Christ* *died for us."* Through Jesus, God gave us a way to be saved from our sins. God showed us His love by giving us the potential for life through the death of His Son, Jesus Christ.

Romans 6:23 *"For the wages of sin is death, but the gift of God is eternal life in Christ Jesus our Lord."* If we remain sinners, we will die. However, if we accept Jesus as our Lord and Savior, and repent of our sins, we will have eternal life.

Romans 10:9-10 *"That if you confess with your mouth the Lord Jesus and believe in your heart that God has raised Him from the dead, you will be saved. For with the heart one believes unto righteousness, and with the mouth confession is made unto salvation."* Just confess that Jesus Christ is Lord and believe in your heart that God raised Him from the dead and you will be saved!

Romans 10:13 *"For whoever calls on the name of the LORD shall be saved."* There are no religious formulas or rituals — Call upon the name of the Lord and you will be saved!

Romans 11:36: *"For of Him and through Him and to Him are all things, to whom be glory forever. Amen."* Determine in your heart to make Jesus Christ the Lord of your life today.

Roman Road: Are You Ready to Accept God's Gift of Salvation?

If you truly believe the message of the Roman Road, and want to accept God's gift of salvation right now, it's a matter of repenting of your sins and turning the rest of your life over to Jesus Christ. Again, this is not a ritual based on any specific words or prayers, but rather, a willful decision and a sincere step of faith.

"Father, I know that I have broken your laws and my sins have separated me from you. I am truly sorry, and now I want to turn away from my past sinful life toward you. Please forgive me, and help me avoid sinning again. I believe that your son, Jesus Christ died for my sins, was resurrected from the dead, is alive, and hears my prayer. I invite Jesus to become the Lord of my life, to rule and reign in my heart from this day forward. Please send your Holy Spirit to help me obey You, and to do Your will for the rest of my life. In Jesus' name I pray, Amen."

"Repent, and let every one of you be baptized in the name of Jesus Christ for the remission of sins; and you shall receive the gift of the Holy Spirit." (Acts 2:38)

If you decided to receive Jesus today, welcome to God's family. Now, as a way to grow closer to Him, the Bible tells us to follow up on our commitment.

- Get <u>baptized</u> as commanded by Christ.
- Tell someone else about your new faith in Christ.
- Spend time with God each day. It does not have to be a long period of time. Just develop the daily habit of praying to Him and reading His Word. Ask God to increase your faith and your understanding of the Bible.

- Seek fellowship with other followers of Jesus. Develop a group of believing friends to answer your questions and support you.
- Find a local church where you can worship God.

www.allaboutgod.com/romanroad.htm
Published by AllaboutGod.com Ministries
M.Houdmann, P. Matthews-Rose, R. Niles, editor.
2002-08
Used by permission.

Questions for the Author

What is the most significant thing you have learned from marathons?

The power I get from faith and prayer to endure to the finish.

What is your favorite motto or quote?

> *"He will give strength to the weary*
> *and increase the power of the weak.*
> *Even youths grow tired and weary,*
> *and young men stumble and fall;*
> *But those who hope in the Lord*
> *will renew their strength.*
> *They will soar on wings like eagles;*
> *they will run and not get weary,*
> *they will walk and not faint."*
> (Isaiah 40:29-31)

What is the most important goal that you would like to accomplish in your life?

Being able to look back at my miles run and remember the people who, because of my faith and witness came to know Jesus as their personal Lord and Savior.

When all is said and done, in what way would you like to be remembered?

I trust that I will be remembered as an encourager who knew Jesus as his personal Savior and was always ready and willing to share with anyone who would listen to, or read about my Christian beliefs; as one who helped some get on the course to heaven's finish line and helped others be better able to 'finish the race' they had already begun. Yes, one who *"ran with perseverance the race that was marked out..."* (Heb. 12:1); and as one who *"finished the race (and) kept the faith."* (2 Tim. 4:7)

After I looked over the questions and answers that I had in my scrapbook, I noticed the following notes and prayer that I had written at the bottom of that page – I believe it closes out nicely the feelings that rest upon my heart for my life's mission and for all Christian runners.

~~~~~~

I am more concerned about what happens during the 'dash period' between the dates that I was 'Born Again' and will crossover the final finish line, than the dash period between the days that I was born and died. The years lived as a Christian, 'Praise the Lord', will be the ones that I will be rewarded for being an *'ambassador..."* *(2 Cor. 5:20)* and was 'Heading Toward the Final Finish Line'.

May this be your prayer: that your feet will be *"...of those who bring good news..."* (Isa. 52:7) and *"...your feet fitted with the readiness that comes from the gospel of peace."* (Eph. 6:15)

If I do not see you on the course, I will see you at the finish line!

Friends Along the Way

Running Clubs
www.team413.org
www.ChristianRunners.org
4 His Temple / www.vandykechurch.org
www.50statesmarathonclub.com
www.50statesanddcmarathongroup.com
www.salisburyrowanrunners.com
www.marathonmaniacs.com
www.tampabayrunners.com
www.manguntrackclub.com

Sports Centers
The Running Center
www.runcenter.com
14308 North Dale Mabry Hwy.
Tampa, FL
(813) 908-1960

FITniche
www.FITniche.com
1421 Town Center Drive
Lakeland, FL
(863)619-5390

Phidippides Sports Center
Carolina Mall
Concord, NC
(704) 786-3312

Ministries
www.lifepoint.tv
www.vandyke.org
www.churchatthemall.net
www.InHisPath.com
www.Oneplace.com
www.crosswalk.com
www.crossway.com
www.SermonSearch.com
www.joyranch.org
www.usfnavs.com
www.moodychurch.org
RunnningToWin@moodychurch.org
(with Dr. Erwin W. Luther)

www.ymca.net
www.Carmen.org
www.AllAboutGOD.com

Photography
asiphoto©
World of Color©
Marathon Foto©
Brightroom Studios, Inc©
Al's Studio of Marion SD©
(www.alsstudioonline.com)
The Denver Post© / Matthew Staver and Lyn Alweis
Steven Yee (Marathon Maniac #1)

Mrs. Diane Gerow
Ms. Annie Leazer
Ms. Lucretia Trent

Drawings
Kourtney Parramore
Janice Coulter
Rrrick Karampatsos
Chr.tripod.com
Unknown Artists

Physicians
Without these dedicated friends, I would have had to train and run in needless extra pain. I highly recommend their services and others like them.

Paton Chiropractic and Sports Medicine
www.PatonChiropractic.com
Certified Athletic Trainer
Lutz, FL 33559
(813) 949-7740

Dr. Richard P. Molloy
Internal Medicine
Tampa, FL 33613
(813) 371-0195

Dr. Bernard F. Germain
(Osteoarthritis)
Tampa, FL 33613
(813) 978-1500

NORTH POINT DENTAL ASSOC.
Tampa, FL
(813) 961-1727

Jeter Chiropractic Clinic
1001 North Main Street
Salisbury, NC
(704) 633-5156

Omni Health Medical Group, P.A.
www.omnihealthmed.com
Concord, NC
(704) 784-4445

Publications
www.running.net (Running Journal ©)
www.MarathonGuide.com
Salisbury Post ©/ Steven Jenkins and Michael
Bostian
Denver Post© / John Meyer Staff Writer
The Abilene Reflector – Chronicle©
The Denver Post© / John Meyer
SRR Club Newsletter

Other References
Wikipedia ® – The Free Encyclopedia – www.
wikipedia.org
GOOGLE ® - www.Google.com

Foundation for American Christian Education©
Noah Webster 1828 Dictionary
www.face.net

RRRICK Karampatsos
613 Sabal Lake Drive
Apt. # 115
Longwood, FL 32779

CPSIA information can be obtained at www.ICGtesting.com
Printed in the USA
BVOW05s0530240215

388981BV00001B/43/P